ISBN 978-1-330-65286-2
PIBN 10087793

This book is a reproduction of an important historical work. Forgotten Books uses
state-of-the-art technology to digitally reconstruct the work, preserving the original format
whilst repairing imperfections present in the aged copy. In rare cases, an imperfection in
the original, such as a blemish or missing page, may be replicated in our edition. We do,
however, repair the vast majority of imperfections successfully; any imperfections that
remain are intentionally left to preserve the state of such historical works.

1 MONTH OF
FREE
READING

at

www.ForgottenBooks.com

By purchasing this book you are eligible for one month membership to ForgottenBooks.com, giving you unlimited access to our entire collection of over 700,000 titles via our web site and mobile apps.

To claim your free month visit:

www.forgottenbooks.com/free87793

English
Français
Deutsche
Italiano
Español
Português

www.forgottenbooks.com

Mythology Photography **Fiction**
Fishing Christianity **Art** Cooking
Essays Buddhism Freemasonry
Medicine **Biology** Music **Ancient
Egypt** Evolution Carpentry Physics
Dance Geology **Mathematics** Fitness
Shakespeare **Folklore** Yoga Marketing
Confidence Immortality Biographies
Poetry **Psychology** Witchcraft
Electronics Chemistry History **Law**
Accounting **Philosophy** Anthropology
Alchemy Drama Quantum Mechanics
Atheism Sexual Health **Ancient History**
Entrepreneurship Languages Sport
Paleontology Needlework Islam
Metaphysics Investment Archaeology
Parenting Statistics Criminology
Motivational

THE SCOT IN ULSTER

SKETCH OF THE
HISTORY OF THE SCOTTISH POPULATION
OF ULSTER

BY

JOHN HARRISON

WILLIAM BLACKWOOD AND SONS
EDINBURGH AND LONDON
MDCCCLXXXVIII

PREFACE.

THESE sketches of the history of the Scottish settlers in Ulster were published in the columns of the 'Scotsman' during this spring. They have been recast, and are now published in a permanent form, as I think they may interest some who care to examine the Irish question for themselves. Their English and Scottish origin seems to me to give to the men of Ulster an inalienable right to protest, as far as they are concerned, against the policy of Separation from Great Britain to which the Irish, —with the genius for nicknames which they possess —at present give the name of Home Rule.

My thanks are due to many friends in Ulster and at home for kind assistance; and more especially to Professor Masson for allowing me to have access to those sheets of the ninth volume of the 'Privy Council Records of Scotland,' now in the press, which bear on the Scottish share in the settlement of 1610.

J. H.

7 GREENHILL PLACE,
EDINBURGH, 16th October 1888.

CONTENTS.

THE SCOT IN ULSTER.

———◆———

CHAPTER I.

THIS is the story of the first great colony which went forth from the "land of brown heath and shaggy wood" in search of a country which would repay the emigrant's toil less grudgingly than did the bare hillsides round the old home. For centuries the Scot had been wont to wander forth over Europe in search of adventure. As a rule, he turned his steps where fighting was to be had, and the pay for killing was reasonably good; for the English wars, while they devastated the country and kept it poor, made the people a nation of soldiers. Others of the race sought fortune in trade instead of in war. The story of these wanderers is known from the history of the Scots Guard, formed from the sur-

A

vivors of that Scottish army which helped so much to win back for France the rich plains of Gascony and Poitou, which the English had held long and firmly; and in the annals of the Scots Brigade, who did such honest, hard fighting among the Dutch dykes against that splendid Spanish infantry which Parma and Spinola led. Often, too, in the chronicles of these centuries, one gets a peep at the Scottish emigrants who had sought their fortune in trade, at Middleburg or Campvere, at Amsterdam or Lubeck, or even among the Tartars in the far-off Baltic Sea. The emigrants who lived out the fighting and the toiling, and settled in these foreign lands, founded families, in whose names may still be traced some faint record of their Scottish origin.

This is, however, the story of a different kind of emigration. These Scots who had flocked from Leith, or Crail, or Berwick to seek fortune, in peace or war, on the continent of Europe, were mostly the young and adventurous, for whom the old home life had become too narrow. They took with them little save their own stout hearts and their national long heads. If they remained permanently in France, or the Low Countries, or Sweden, they married from the people of their adopted land, and the blood of their descendants became less and less Scottish as the generations followed each other. The time arrived at last, however, when war with England ceased, and internal strife became less bloody, and Scotland began to be too small for her rapidly growing population, for in those days food did not necessarily come where there were mouths to consume it. Then the Scots, true to the race from which they spring—for "Norman, and Saxon, and Dane are we"—began to go forth, like the northern hordes in days of yore, the women and the children along with the bread-winners, and crossed the seas, and settled in new lands, and were "fruitful, and multiplied and replenished the earth," until the globe is circled round with colonies which are of our blood, and which love and cherish the old "land of the mountain and the flood." It was in the beginning of the seventeenth century that the first of these swarms crossed the narrowest of the seas which surround Scotland; it went out from the Ayrshire and Galloway ports, and settled in the north of Ireland. The numbers which went were large. They left Scotland at a time when she was deeply moved by the great Puritan revival. They took with them their Scottish character and their Scottish Calvinism. They founded the Scottish colony in Ulster. Thus it comes to pass "that the foundation of Ulster society is Scottish. It is the solid granite on which it rests."[1] The history of this Scottish colony seems worth telling, for it is a story of which any Scotsman at home or abroad may be proud. Its early history is quaint and interesting; there is much of suffering and oppression in the story of the succeeding years, but there are flashes of bright-

[1] See an article in 'Fraser's Magazine' on "Ulster," July-December 1876, p. 220.

ness to relieve the gloom. The men which this race
of Scotsmen has produced are worthy of the parent
stock; the contribution which this branch of the
Scottish nation has made to the progress of civilisation proves that it has not forgotten the old ideals;
the portion of Ireland which these Scotsmen hold is
so prosperous and contented that it permits our
statesmen to forget that it is a part of that most
" distressful " country.

Our story opens in the days when the world was
young to the nations who had embraced the Reformation; for they to whom it had been given to see
that new vision of God, conceived also a new ideal
of life. Then all things seemed possible to men of
daring, because the old limits in both the physical
and the moral worlds had been found to be but the
invention of man, and the universe was to be, for all
time coming, limitless. It was the world in which
Shakespeare and Bacon had grown up; in which
Spenser had sung of love and purity; in which
Sidney had acted his gallant part, and died his
chivalrous death; in which William the Silent, and
Knox, and Cecil had toiled that we might live in
freedom and light. It was an age in which single
men with strangely inadequate means dared great
deeds, which read to us now like fables; when a
young adventurer set sail from Plymouth in a ship
little bigger than a big herring-boat, and waged war
against the greatest monarch in the world, and plun-

dered all his colonies along the Pacific shore, and sailed round the world on his way home with a million sterling worth of plunder; and when another young skipper, in five of those queer old tubs which still float on the Zuyder Zee, went out into the wonder-haunted East, and conquered a New Holland greater than the old, in case it were necessary to break the dykes and leave the old land—to give Holland to the ocean rather than to the Spaniard. It was the age in which the individual was strong and the State weak ; in which strong men trusted in their own strength, and did the work of the State.

And now Queen Elizabeth, who had been the strange, fickle, uncertain, and yet withal the luminous sun in that great English world, was dead, and the fashion of the time was to change. Still, for a while her methods were followed, for the spirit of the great Elizabethan age survived, although its sun had set—still it was left to the individual to do the work of the State. One of the enterprises which occupied the adventurous spirits of the kingdom during the early years of James I.'s reign was the colonisation of Ulster, and in this the Scots took their full share.

The last years of Elizabeth's reign had been disturbed by the rebellion of the great Earl of Tyrone, who, as The O'Neill, claimed to be King of Ulster. Tyrone fought a good fight—it is not here necessary to inquire why he rebelled. He defeated the first English commander who went against him; and cajoled the Earl of Essex, who next opposed him, into making terms, which Elizabeth at once refused to ratify.   He then obtained assistance from Spain, and a Spanish force actually landed at Kinsale. This small army, as well as Tyrone's larger following, was, however, defeated by Lord Mountjoy, who succeeded Essex as Deputy.   The Spaniards gladly returned home, and Tyrone submitted.   So in the end of 1602, a few weeks before Elizabeth's death, the war, which had lasted from 1596, came to an end.   Tyrone promised to be for the future a faithful subject; he received pardon for his treason, and was reinstated in his land.   There was peace in Ireland; but Tyrone had shown what "The O'Neill" could do, when he happened to be an able man: he had united the tribes of Ulster against the English, and had shaken the English Government in Ireland to its foundation.

About this time one of the cadets of the great O'Neill family, who rejoiced in the euphonious if somewhat cumbersome name of "Con M'Neale M'Bryan Feartagh O'Neal," got into trouble, out of which he seemed to be likely to escape only with the loss of his head.[1]   He ruled the Upper Clannaboye, the north half of County Down, now the most Scottish part of Ireland, and he lived in the old house of Castlereagh, a name which has since be-

---

[1] The account of the settlement of County Down is taken from 'The Montgomery MSS., Belfast, 1869,' and from 'The Hamilton MSS., Belfast, 1867.'

come well known in English history. In the end
of 1602, when Queen Elizabeth lay dying, Con
happened to be holding high state in his halls of
Castlereagh with his brothers, and cousins, and
relatives of near degree. They were all "proper"
men—to use a Celtic term of respect—and quite
naturally drank Con's cellar dry; whereupon the
chief despatched retainers to Belfast, two miles distant, for a fresh supply of wine. How there was
wine at Belfast we do not know, for it was then
scarcely even a hamlet.[1] There his servants had a
quarrel with certain English soldiers, and came back
to their master's castle without the "drink." This
roused Con to fury, and he threatened dire ven-
geance on his clansmen if they did not return to
the fight, punish the English, and recover the wine.
The second encounter was more serious than the
first; an English soldier was killed; and the Irish
Government took the matter up. O'Neills were not
just at this time popular with the ruling powers; so
Con's offence, which at another time might have
been passed over as a most legitimate after-dinner
frolic for an Irish gentleman of quality, was termed
"levying war against the Queen." Con was thrown
into Carrickfergus Castle, the strongest fort in
Ulster; and Sir Arthur Chichester, who was the
most powerful Englishman in the North, proposed
in a letter still extant to hang Con, without troubling
him with a trial or waiting for leave from the Lord-

[1] History of Belfast, by George Benn, p. 76.

Deputy.[1] In this desperate plight Con found a "ministering angel" in his wife, and Lady Con discovered a friend who, for a "consideration," was willing to lend his assistance, and who fortunately proved just the kind of ally that was needed. This "disinterested friend" was Hugh Montgomery, the laird of Braidstane, in Ayrshire. Montgomery was sprung from a collateral branch of the noble house of Eglinton, and like so many of the lesser Scottish gentry of the period, had sought his fortune on the Continent, and seen service under Prince Maurice of Orange, in Holland. He was a capable man, whose wits had been sharpened by being compelled to discover means of escape out of troubles into which his hot blood had led him; he had been looking out for an eligible "settlement" in the north of Ireland, and kept himself aware of what went on there through relatives who traded to Ireland from the port of Irvine. Montgomery arranged for Con's rescue from Carrickfergus Castle. The plan was on the same lines as that by which he himself had a few years before effected his escape from the Binnenhof, the old palace and fortress of The Hague, well known to all visitors to Holland. The laird of Braidstane had become too eminently respectable a personage to carry out the design himself; besides, he was married now, and his wife may have had some foolish feminine prejudices against her husband doing love-making. He therefore intrusted the carrying out of the enter-

[1] Calendar of State Papers, Ireland, 1603-6, p. 156.

prise to a relative, Thomas Montgomery of Black-
ston, who was owner of a sloop which sometimes
traded with Carrickfergus. The said Thomas proceeded to make love to the daughter of the keeper
of Carrickfergus Castle, and became a great favourite
with the household ; and, like a generous fellow as he
was, he at all times was ready to give the guard as
much drink as they cared for. So it came to pass that
love-making and wine somewhat discomposed the discipline of Carrickfergus Castle—even to this day the
discipline of Irish jails is said to be somewhat loose.
Con was furnished with a rope by which he let himself out of his window, found Thomas Montgomery's
sloop waiting for him, and himself in the good house
of Braidstane, within a few hours. To Thomas's
honour it must be recorded that he did really marry
the jailer's daughter, "called Annas Dobbin, whom
I have often seen and spoken with, for she lived in
Newtown till anno 1664."

Arrived at Braidstane, Con entered into an agreement by which he ceded half his lands in Clannaboye to Montgomery, on condition that the latter
obtained a free pardon from King James for all his
offences, and got him admitted to kiss the King's
hand. This indenture was believed to have been
"fully indorsed and registered in the Town Councill
book of the royal burgh of Air or Irvine."[1] The
entry, however, has never been discovered in the
Town Council records of these burghs. Mont-

[1] Montgomery MSS., p. 28.

gomery set to work to fulfil his part of the agreement, with the help of his brother, who held position at Court; but his influence proving insufficient, he was compelled to have recourse to another Scot, whose word had more weight with the King. This "kindly brother Scot" was James Hamilton, who had settled in Dublin some years before the Union as a schoolmaster. He had been employed by James VI. as a political agent for various purposes, and especially to gain the adhesion of the Irish leaders to James's claims to the crown of the United Kingdom. Hamilton's influence proved sufficiently potent. Con was admitted to the royal presence, and kissed the King's hand, received pardon for the offences of himself and his kinsmen, and returned in triumph to his ancestral halls of Castlereagh. Yes; but a new agreement had been found necessary, and poor Con's lands had to be made broad enough to satisfy James Hamilton as well as Hugh Montgomery. So, on the 16th April 1605, letters-patent were issued under the Great Seal, " on the humble petition of Conn M'Neale M'Bryan Feartagh O'Neale, and of Hugh Montgomery, Esq., and of James Hamilton, Esq.," granting to the said James Hamilton all the lands in the Upper Clannaboye and the Great Ards which had been possessed by Con or by his father, Bryan Feartagh O'Neale, in his lifetime. Hamilton became bound to "plant" the lands with English and Scottish colonists, and to grant them only to those of English and Scottish blood, "and

O'Neale and his heirs)."[1]   Thus this great tract of
land, the northern half of County Down, was handed
over to Hamilton, who had before entered into
agreement with Montgomery and O'Neill as to what
portion he should retain, what share Hugh Montgomery should receive, and how much of his ancestral
estate should be restored to Con O'Neill.

It is a strange story, but thoroughly characteristic
of the time; for it was a period in which popular
feeling was singularly inert, the Reformation fire
having burned down, and the great Puritan revival
not yet arrived.   The affairs of the country were
therefore "arranged" by King James, with the assistance of a knot of courtiers—shrewd, keen men,
without any very high sense of the beauty of unself-
ishness.   There is no doubt, too, that the main
points in the story are strictly true, and the principal
actors are real figures in history.   James Hamilton
became first Sir James and then Viscount Clannaboye, a title now borne by his descendant, the late
Viceroy of India, Lord Dufferin and Clannaboye.
Montgomery became Lord Montgomery of the Ards,
and although the peerage has become extinct, the
Montgomerys still hold a portion of the land which
they acquired at this time, and still bury among the
romantic ruins of Grey Abbey.   Con soon managed
to run through his property, and disappears from history: but his son Daniel fought for Charles I.; went
into exile with Charles II.; returned with him; mar-

---

[1] Calendar of State Papers, Ireland, 1603-6, p. 271; also
see 'Miscellany of the Abbotsford Club,' p. 270.

ried the Countess of Chesterfield, and died at the English Court in 1663, wealthy and honoured.[1]

It must be noted that the idea of planting colonies in Ireland from the neighbouring island was not a new one. Again and again, during Elizabeth's reign, schemes of colonisation had been drawn up, but these had as a rule failed because the men chosen to carry them out were of the wrong stamp. This was not even the first attempt to "plant" the southern shore of Belfast Lough, for it had been granted thirty years before to Sir Thomas Smith, but he had been driven out by the O'Neills. The grant to Smith in 1579, like those given thirty years later by James I., aimed at a thorough colonisation of the country, for he was bound "to enter in with a power of natural Englishmen," and "to divide the lands with such as hazard themselves, or aid with men and money."[2] The Earl of Essex next tried his fortune, and failed. The settlement succeeded now for two reasons: first, because King James's Government was so strong that it could keep the peace even in Ireland; and secondly, because Scotsmen had been for nearly a generation deprived of their wonted occupation of civil war, and therefore had taken the "itch" for emigration. As soon as County Down was opened up, colonists flocked across, until the district became Scottish.

[1] Benn's History of Belfast, p. 77.
[2] History of the County of Down, by Alexander Knox, M.D. Dublin, 1875.

CHAPTER II.

THE SCOT SETTLES NORTH DOWN AND COUNTY ANTRIM.

TWO miles south from Donaghadee, on the shore road into the Upper Ards, that narrow peninsula between Strangford Lough and the Irish Sea, there lies a little enclosure which must arrest the stranger's attention. It is a graveyard, and is called Templepatrick. It is surrounded by low stone walls; no church or temple is now within its confines; no trees or flowers give grateful shade, or lend colour and tender interest; it is thickly covered with green mounds, and with monumental slabs of grey slaty stone,—the graves are packed close together. Read the simple "headstones," and you discover no trace of sentiment; few fond and loving words; no request for the prayers of the passer-by for the souls of those who sleep below; nothing more akin to sentiment than "Sacred to the memory of." Above, great masses of grey clouds, as they go scudding past, throw down on the traveller, as he rests and thinks, big drops of rain; and before him is spread out, north, south, and east, the sullen sea, whose moan fills all his sense of hearing. It is not the spot which a man would love to picture to himself as his last resting-place. Read the names on the stones, and you discover why here in Ireland there is to be found nothing of tender grace to mark the higher side, nothing of tinsel to show the lower, of Irish character. The names are very Scottish—such as Andrew Byers, John Shaw, Thomas M'Millan, Robert Angus; it is a burying-place of the simple peasants of County Down, who are still, in the end of the nineteenth century, as Scottish as they were when they landed here nearly three centuries ago.

These graveyards of the Scots are now on every shore,—among the great forests of Canada, as well as here by the side of the Irish Sea; where the new Dunedin rises out of the Southern Ocean, as well as in the old Dunedin, under the shadow of its Castle rock. Thus enter into a common rest those who shared a common toil, whether in the old motherland, or far away scattered over the wide world. Why should they indulge in sentiment in death who have known only stern toil in life?—for them is more fitting some expression of that high faith which they have kept, even though they may in holding it have made it somewhat unlovely. And what recks it, after all, to the Scot whether he sleep in an unknown grave, as sleeps John Knox, beside the "great kirk" of Edinburgh, which had so often resounded with his eloquence; or, like Scott, rest, where he desired to rest, among the ruins of Dryburgh Abbey; or, like that other sweet singer of our Border-land, lie far away from the sound of his dearly-loved Teviot, where

"A distant and a deadly shore has Leyden's cold remains."

It is enough if he have done the work which his hand found to do, whether it be, like Knox's, the building up of a nation's character, or, like these peasants, but the tilling of thirty acres of not too fertile land in County Down.

The stuff of which the great body of the emigrants was made formed one element in the success of the colony, the other was the character of the two men who led and controlled them.

Had the system of "cram" been invented in James I.'s time, and had the two men on whom devolved the colonisation of South Clannaboye and the Great Ards been chosen by the most exhausting of Civil Service examinations, it is somewhat doubtful whether our modern system of discovering administrators would have put forward men so well fitted for the work as Hamilton and Montgomery. Both seem to have possessed those qualities, amiable and unamiable, which go to make up the very successful man. Montgomery, too, as the chroniclers tell us, was supported by an able and active wife— a requisite for successful colonial governors, which

the authorities have not yet, as far as has been reported, attempted to discover by competitive exam-
ination.   Each of the two "adventurers," as soon as
his patent was passed by the Irish Council, crossed
into Scotland to call upon his whole kith and kin to
aid him in his great scheme.   Both were Ayrshire
men, and both from the northern division of the
county.   Hamilton was a "son of the manse" of
Dunlop; and still the curious may see the quaint
monument which he raised to the memory of his
father and mother in the kirkyard of Dunlop, within
a stonethrow of the railway between Kilmarnock and
Glasgow.   Montgomery was one of the great Ayrshire family of that name, and sixth laird of Braidstane, near Beith.   It is well to note that matters
were differently managed in the beginning of the
seventeenth century from what they are in the end of
the nineteenth.   Nowadays, Hamilton and Montgomery would have an interview with some enterprising firm of accountants in Glasgow, who would
thereafter issue a circular citing the Limited Liability
Acts of Victoria, and calling on all sensible people to
take advantage of the enormous power of developing
wealth possessed by the lands of Con O'Neill, Esq.,
by taking shares in an Upper Clannaboye Land
Colonisation Company, Limited.   In those old days
the two "undertakers" had to rely on their own
resources, and on the assistance which their Ayrshire
friends were able and willing to give them.

It must be kept in remembrance that Hamilton

received the grant of Irish land on the express condition that he should "plant" it with Scottish and
English colonists. We know generally how he im-
plemented his bargain. He seems to have received
the hearty support of his own family, for four of his
five brothers aided his enterprise, and shared his
prosperity: from them are descended numerous
families in Ulster, and at least two Irish noble
families. Further, there is no doubt that Hamilton
did "plant" the land which he had acquired with
Scottish tenants, and administered his great estate
with prudence and ability. There are recorded the
names of those who held farms from Hamilton, and
good Scottish surnames they are, and evidently from
the same country as the men whom we shall find
followed Montgomery. Hamilton founded the towns
of Bangor and Killyleagh, in County Down. It is
mentioned, too, that he attended to spiritual things,
for he raised churches in each of the six parishes
embraced in his estate—Bangor, Killinchy, Holywood, Ballyhalbert, Dundonald, and Killyleagh.
He "made it his business to bring very learned
and pious ministers out of Scotland, and planted all
the parishes of his estate." Moreover, we discover
how primitive were the times in which the Lord
Clannaboye lived, for we read "that he maintained
the ministers liberally, received even their public re-
proofs submissively, and had secret friendly corre-
spondence with them."[1]

[1] Hamilton MSS., p. 33.

To Hamilton fell the western portion of North Down, to Montgomery the eastern, and both seem to have added to their estates, as Con O'Neill was forced to sell the third, which he had reserved for himself. There is preserved an exceedingly careful account of how Hugh Montgomery "planted" his estate—the country round Newtown and Donagh-adee, known as the Great Ards. Montgomery belonged to a family having numerous connections throughout North Ayrshire and Renfrewshire, and to them he turned for assistance. His principal supporters were his kinsman Thomas Montgomery, who had done the successful wooing at Carrickfergus; his brother-in-law, John Shaw, younger son of the laird of Wester Greenock; and Colonel David Boyd, of the noble house of Kilmarnock. With their help he seems to have persuaded many others of high and low degree to join in trying their fortune in Ireland. The names of the emigrants are intensely Scottish [1]— Montgomeries and Calderwoods, Agnews and Adairs, Cunninghams and Shaws and Muirs, Maxwells and Boyles and Harvies, and many others with good west-country surnames. They began to cross in May 1606, and found the country "more wasted than America (when the Spaniards landed there)," for between Donaghadee and Newtown "thirty cabins could not be found, nor any stone walls, but ruined, roofless churches, and a few vaults at Grey Abbey, and a stump of an old castle at Newtown." [2] The

[1] Montgomery MSS., p. 56, note.   [2] Ibid., p. 58.

war with Tyrone had been conducted with such savage cruelty on both sides, that great tracts of country had been reduced to a desert, and this district seems to have been one which had been swept bare of inhabitants.

The colonists were of very various ranks of life, and of varied experience, probably most of them accustomed to farming and agricultural work; but the chronicler tells too of "smiths, masons, and carpenters. I knew many of them, old men when I was a boy at school, and had little employments for some of them."[1] They crossed in the early spring of 1606, and their first work was to build cottages and booths for themselves of sods and saplings of ashes, with rushes for thatch, and to make the "stump of a castle" at Newtown fit to shelter Sir Hugh and his wife and family. They then proceeded to break up the ground and plant crops. The soil, which had lain fallow for some years, yielded abundantly, so that "the harvests of 1606 and 1607 stocked the people with grain, for the lands were never naturally so productive since that time."[2] These plentiful seasons gave the colony a great impetus, as there was plenty, not only for home consumption, but for sale to new-comers. Besides, the tidings of success of course induced others to follow, for it would immediately become known along the Scottish shore that the first emigrants were comfortably settled in their new country, and that there was

[1] Montgomery MSS., p. 59.   [2] Ibid., p. 62.

every prospect of the colony succeeding. With the
vigour characteristic of the race, the new colonists
soon established themselves firmly in their new home,
and the face of the country assumed a different appearance from the desolation it had before presented.
The town of Newtown grew up round the "stump of
a castle," while Sir Hugh Montgomery transformed
the ruin into a great country-house. In 1613 letters-
patent were issued creating Newtown a borough, with
provost and burgesses, and with right to send two
members to the Parliament at Dublin. Before many
years were over, Newtown proudly boasted of a
market-cross, "an excellent piece of freestone work
of eight squares," with stair leading to a platform,
where proclamations were made, and from which, on
very festive occasions, claret ran, just as was the custom at the Cross of Edinburgh at this very time. At
the present time Newtown, now known as Newtown-
Ards, is a clean, thriving little town of 9000 inhabitants, with broad streets, and just enough linen
manufacturing going on to keep the people busy;
while it is famed for the culture of roses all over the
three kingdoms.

Sir Hugh was not unmindful of the spiritual affairs
of the colony. He had brought with him "two or
three chaplains for his parishes;" and one of his
first cares was to proceed to rebuild the ruined
church of Newtown. In this work he was assisted
by the "general free contribution of the planters,
some with money, others with handycrafts, and many

with labouring," so that before the winter of 1607 the church was ready for service.[1] Perhaps it is one of the most remarkable and most striking features of this Scottish colony in Ulster, that it was from the first, and has remained even through many persecutions, so consistently and so strongly Presbyterian. The Presbyterianism of the colonists was a strange comment on the apparent success of King James in Scotland ; for during these very years (from 1607 onwards) it appeared as if the King was going to realise the dream of his life—the establishment of Episcopacy in his native country.[2] The back of the Presbyterian Church seemed broken, and the King was steadily introducing Episcopalian forms of worship. It becomes apparent how "skin-deep" and unnatural the change in Scotland must have been, to find that these Scottish colonists set up for themselves the Presbyterian worship in Ireland, although there the Established Church was Episcopalian. The clergy seem either to have come with the colonists, as in the case of Sir Hugh Montgomery's "plantation," or to have been "called" as soon as the Scots were sufficiently settled to be able to form a congregation and build a church. Ulster Presbyterianism was not, however, altogether derived from Scotland. A considerable portion of the English colonists, especially those who came to the London settle-

[1] Montgomery MSS., p. 61.
[2] Register of the Privy Council of Scotland, vol. viii., Pref. xviii.

ment in Londonderry county, were Puritans, and joined with the Scots in Church affairs. A strong Calvinistic element was also afterwards infused into the district by the French Huguenots, who settled in different parts of Ireland after the Revocation of the Edict of Nantes. From the settlement which they made at Lisburn, Ulster derived much of her pre-eminence in the linen manufacture. Many French names thus introduced are still to be found in Ulster.

The foundations of the industries of Ulster were laid by Montgomery, who was assisted in this work by his wife. The productiveness of the first harvests caused Lady Montgomery to build water-mills in all the parishes, which did away with the use of the native "quairn stones." Her ladyship had also farms at Newtown and Grey Abbey and Comber, which gave employment to the emigrants who had not capital enough to start small farms. To these cottagers she gave grass for a cow and sheep, and a plot for flax and potatoes. She also encouraged the spinning and weaving both of linen and wool; and shortly the people were able to weave their own "breakin," and to dress in homespun, as they had been wont to do in their native Ayrshire. This wearing of the Scottish "breakin," which was either tartan, or more likely a kind of "shepherd check," was afterwards alleged as a reproach against these Ulster Scots in the English Parliament, in the course of a debate on 3d December 1656. "For in the north the Scotch keep up an interest distinct in garb and all formalities, and are able to raise an army of 40,000 fighting men at any time.[1] A market was established at Newtown, which soon became a place of resort, both for the people of the surrounding country, and also for merchants from the Scottish coast, who crossed to it from Stranraer and Portpatrick. Many of the wealthier class of colonists too, it is recorded, began to act as merchants and carry on business with the continents. " They built stone houses, and they traded, to enable them to buy lands, to France, Flanders, Norway, &c., as they still do."

The success of this settlement made by Hamilton and Montgomery was immediate; for four years after the foundation of the colony—in 1610—Montgomery alone was able to bring before "the King's muster-master a thousand able fighting men to serve, when out of them a militia should be raised."[2] Four years later, we have again specific information of the progress of the Scottish colonies under Hamilton and Montgomery. It is contained in a letter from the Earl of Abercorn to John Murray, King James's Secretary of State. Abercorn had been called in to act as arbiter between Hamilton and Montgomery, who were constantly quarrelling about boundaries, Con O'Neill's estate being by this time pretty well absorbed. He writes: "They have above 2000 habile Scottis men weill armit heir, rady for his

---

[1] Montgomery MSS., p. 65, note.   [2] Ibid., p. 66.

Majestie's service as thai sall be commandit." "Sir
Hew Montgomerie is in building ane fyin houese at
the Newton, quhairof ane quarter is almost compleit,
an Sir James hes buildit at Killilarche ane very
stronge castill, the lyk is not in the northe."[1] This
muster of 2000 men able to bear arms, of course
represented an emigration of at least 10,000 souls.
Even now, after this long interval of time, it is cheer-
ing to read of any success being accomplished at
any period in Ireland, and it is not surprising that
the old historian of the colony should have broken
forth into singing. "Now everybody minded their
trades, and the plough and the spade, building and
setting fruit-trees, &c., in orchards and gardens, and
by ditching in their grounds. The old women spun,
and the young girls plyed their nimble fingers at
knitting, and everybody was innocently busy. Now
the golden peaceable age renewed; no strife, contention, querulous lawyers, or Scottish or Irish feuds
between clans and families and sirnames."[2] Verily
it must have been a golden age which had dawned
on one sea-washed corner of unhappy Ireland.

Meantime, across the river Lagan, in County
Antrim, a "plantation" had been made which, although not at first peculiarly Scottish, was soon to
become so. During almost the whole of James's
reign probably the most powerful man in Ireland was
Sir Arthur Chichester, who in 1604 became Lord-

[1] State Papers of James VI. (Abbotsford Club), pp. 233, 234.
[2] Montgomery MSS., p. 66.

Deputy, an office which he held until 1616. He was an exceedingly able and resolute man, a faithful servant of the King, but one who never lost sight of his own advantage. In the distribution of lands which took place during his term of office, he shared largely; but even before he became Deputy he had received a piece of land which is still in the hands of his descendant, the Marquis of Donegal. In 1603 Chichester obtained a grant of "the castle of Bealfaste or Belfast, with the appurtenants and hereditaments, spiritual and temporal, situate in the Lower Clandeboye;"[1] while in the years immediately succeeding he acquired the lands along the north shore of what was then called Carrickfergus Bay almost to Lough Larne. There seems to have been an old castle, in a tumble-down condition—as most things were in this part of the country—at Belfast, when Chichester got the lands, and probably a hamlet, but it was a place of no importance. Belfast is in reality, from its very foundation, not an Irish, but an English and Scottish town. Chichester was too busy with the affairs of the State to attend to "planting" his allotment of land, so he contented himself with building a great house, and let his lands on long leases, largely to the officers of his army, so that they might do duty for him. The survey of 1611 tells us how the settlement was progressing. What is now covered by the southern portion of Belfast had been leased by Chichester for sixty-one years, at £10 per annum,

[1] Benn's History of Belfast, p. 78.

to Moses Hill, "sometime lieutenant of his horse-troop." From this Moses Hill is descended the Marquis of Downshire. Hill was busy building a new castle on the site of the old ruin, for the defence of the ford on the river Lagan, and near it "the town of Belfast is plotted out in a good forme, wherein are many famelyes of English, Scotch, and some Manks-men already inhabitinge, and ane inn with very good lodginge, which is a great comforte to the travellers in these partes." The Settlement Commissioners passed along the north shore of Belfast Lough, find-ing everywhere houses springing up, and in every part of the Lord-Deputy's lands "many English fame-lies, some Scottes, and dyvers cyvill Irish planted."[1] At Carrickfergus the Commissioners found a pier and town-wall being built, and all through South Antrim —in island Magee, at Templepatrick, at Massereene, and along the shores of Lough Neagh to Toome— settlements of English and Scots, and houses and "bawns" being erected.[2] While South Antrim was thus "planted" mainly by English settlers, the north-ern half of the county was opened up for settlement, without the violent transference of land from Celt to Saxon which was carried out in other parts of Ulster. The north-east corner of Ireland had been long held by the Macdonnels, a clan which also peopled the island of Jura, and Cantyre on the mainland of Scot-land. The chief of these Scoto-Irishmen, Randal Macdonnel, after Tyrone's rebellion, resolved to throw

[1] Benn's History of Belfast, p. 86.   [2] Ibid., pp. 674-676.

in his lot with the Government, and turn loyal subject. He persevered in this course, notwithstanding many trials to his loyalty, and as reward he received a grant of the northern half of County Antrim, from Larne to Portrush, and the honour of knighthood. He set himself ardently to the improvement of his lands, " letting out to the natives on the coast, and also to the Scottish settlers, such arable portions of his lands as had been depopulated by the war, for terms varying from 21 to 301 years."[1] These leases seem to have been largely taken advantage of by the Scottish settlers, who allowed the natives to keep the "Glynnes" or Glens—that district so much visited now for its splendid coast scenery—and themselves took possession of the rich land along the river Bann, from Lough Neagh to the town of Coleraine near its mouth. So Macdonnel and his property prospered; and in 1620, when King James raised him to the dignity of Earl of Antrim, the patent conferring the honour, after enumerating the faithful services which Macdonnel had rendered to the Crown, specially mentioned "the fact of his having strenuously exerted himself in settling British subjects on his estates."[2] Thus County Antrim, from north to south, became nearly as Scottish as the portion of County Down north of the Mourne mountains.

[1] The Macdonnels of Antrim, by the Rev. George Hill, p. 229.
[2] Ibid., p. 231.

CHAPTER III.

THE GREAT PLANTATION IN ULSTER.

IT is beyond measure refreshing, after toiling through tiresome volumes in which a narrow streamlet of text finds its way through a perfect quagmire of notes, and which are so full of facts that they conceal the truth, to turn from them and let the eye wander through some chapters of 'The Fortunes of Nigel.' It is like a draught of sparkling ale after a long and dusty tramp : life comes dancing back again through the veins ; the eye once more has power to enjoy the glare of heaven's light. The weary mind is in touch with something human ; it realises the fact that the men who made history in James I.'s time were made of flesh and blood ; that they did not act like machines, but were partly good and partly bad—certainly not the fiends that Irish patriots have painted, devouring the innocent chiefs of Ulster, who, it must be understood, need to be pictured like lambs in one of Caldecott's picture-books, walking on their hind legs, with pink ribbons round their necks. Read 'The Fortunes of Nigel,' and you understand the part which the Scots took in the great plantation in Ulster; you comprehend, in a measure, the misshapen little king, although you probably undervalue his practical ability, when he chose to apply himself to business; and you see the poverty of the old land north of the Tweed, and the neediness of the flock of supplicants who followed James to London,—"wheresoever the carcass is, there will the eagles be gathered together." As in a mirror, too, you see the baneful power of the royal favourites, who lived and had their being by reason of James's vanity and laziness. One sighs in vain for some similar guiding light to assist in the understanding of the men who made history in Ireland; for it is strange that in a country which is bubbling over with humour, the writers on history seem to divide themselves into the stupid people who try to write the truth, and do it stupidly, and the clever people, who do not much trouble to seek the draw-well in which truth takes refuge. And yet the men who played the great parts in this strange drama cannot have been dull uninteresting men. We know partly what the leaders of the English interest were,—Chichester, Carew, Davies,—and they have in them that mixture of good and bad parts which tempts the pencil of the historical painter. Even after kneeling in alabaster in the little church of Carrickfergus for two centuries and a half, with no company but his

wife and baby, Chichester looks a capable, many-
sided man, in whom there must have been the play
of light and shade. But what the Irish chiefs were
who made so strange an exit from their own land we
know not, unless we are able to believe the theory
that they were innocent lambs, who always wore
pretty bows of pink ribbon. It is unfortunate that
no Irishman has arisen with the deep historical knowledge, the strong sympathy with the past, the sunny
humour, and the splendid imagination of Sir Walter
Scott, to throw the clear noonday light of genius on
the dark places of the path—to illumine the Ireland
of Chichester, as Scott has made bright the England
of James I. and Salisbury.

There is much material recently made available,
by the publication of the Irish State Papers, for
forming some conception of Ireland in the beginning
of the seventeenth century. One thing is very evident—that the English and Scots of the time looked
on the Irish just as the white settlers regard Kaffirs
in Cape Colony. In the official documents they are
invariably termed the "mere Irish." They were
treated as an inferior and subject race, who would
do a graceful act if they would only disappear from
history. The official reports by Government servants
made in the end of the sixteenth and beginning of
the seventeenth century, also give clear and vivid
pictures of the state of Ulster. They may be taken
as essentially correct, as the writers had means of
observing, and no reasons for writing anything that

was not true. Ulster is always spoken of as the most savage part of Ireland. At the beginning of James I.'s time, although Elizabeth had waged fierce and devastating wars against the Ulster chiefs during most of her long reign, English authority was scarcely recognised in the north of Ireland. It was represented by the commanders of the ten districts into which Ulster was divided; but their rule was little more than a military one, and scarce extended beyond the buildings which composed their military posts,[1] and by the bishops of the Episcopal Church, who had probably even fewer followers in spiritual things than the district governors had in temporal. The country still enjoyed its native laws and customs—still obeyed its native chiefs. There were no towns in Ireland to play the part which the English and Scottish burghs had done in the middle ages, to be the homes of free institutions, the centres from which civilisation might spread. Belfast scarcely existed even in name, and Derry and Carrickfergus consisted but of small collections of houses round the English forts. The whole country, like our Scottish Highlands, was inhabited by clansmen, obeying tribal laws and usages, and living in some measure on agriculture, but mainly on the produce of their herds and flocks. The land was held by the chiefs nominally for the clans, but really for their own benefit. The tillers of the soil had no sure hold over the lands which they worked, " no certain portion of land

[1] Calendar of State Papers, Ireland, 1608-10, p. xxiv.

being let to any tenant;"[1] so that "the more careful and industrious the tenant, the more liable to
oppression of all kinds—the more likely to be turned
out of his holding."[2]   In fact, the chief might de-
prive the clansman of his holding, just as the clansman might pass from one chief to another.[3]   Rent
was paid to the chief mainly in kind—in oats, oat-
meal, butter, hogs, and mutton ; partly in money, the
amount of cash paid depending on the number of
cattle fed.[4]   Nor was the civic rule more satisfactory
than the land tenure.   The different clans of Ulster
recognised the chief of the great O'Neill family as
King of Ulster, when " The O'Neill " of the time was
strong enough to enforce his claims.   The chiefs of
all the clans and septs of clans seem to have been
elected from the families of the chiefs—all the sons,
legitimate and illegitimate, and the brothers of the
deceased being eligible.[5]   A vacancy was therefore
the signal for fierce contention, which frequently
ended in faction-fight, and almost certainly in one
party intriguing with the English authorities, to whom
he promised faithful allegiance—a promise surely
broken when the end of the assistance was attained.
In addition, as was the fact in our Scottish Highlands, clan hatred and war between the clans was
common ; for each chief had his body-guard of

---

[1] Calendar of State Papers, Ireland, 1608-10, p. 534.
[2] Ibid., Carew, 1603-24, p. xiv.
[3] Ibid., Ireland, 1608-10, p. 534.   [4] Ibid.
[5] Ibid., Carew, 1603-24, p. xx.   Also Sir Henry Maine's
Early Law and Custom, p. 136.

" swordsmen "—the cadets of the noble houses, who were far too noble to labour, and had therefore to be provided with fighting, and with plunder too, which it was preferable to take from men of another name rather than from the humble members of their own clan.[1] Readers are very much accustomed at present to be served with roseate pictures of the happiness of Irish pastoral life before the " black shadow" of English rule fell on it. To those who enjoy such imaginative writing, the summing up of the men who have laboured to calendar the Irish State Papers will sound cold and hard and unsympathetic. " In all the State Papers the system is represented as resulting, for the tenants, in the most painful uncertainty of tenure and great social insecurity and discontent. In a political point of view the result was most formidable to the English interest, as it rendered the Creaghts (the wandering herdsmen) entirely dependent on the heads of the sept and the inferior chiefs, and placed the whole power of the community unreservedly in their chief's hands for all purposes of war or of peace."[2] It is evident too, that, although the long wars of the sixteenth century had not tended to civilise Ulster, they had had the baneful effect of desolating it to a frightful extent; for both sides conducted the war with terrible cruelty, so that the accounts of the ruin of

[1] Calendar of State Papers, Carew, p. xl. Also, Curte's History, vol. i. p. 13.
[2] Ibid., Ireland, 1608-10, p. xxviii.

the country and the loss of population are most heartrending. All authorities agree that there were great tracts of country, once fruitful, now uncultivated and without population.

The plantations in County Down and County Antrim, thorough as they were as far as they went, were limited in scope in comparison with the "Great Plantation in Ulster," for which James I.'s reign will be for ever remembered in Ireland. It is extremely difficult to make out the circumstances which led up to this remarkable measure, or to understand the action of the Ulster chiefs, who, to all appearance, played so thoroughly into the hands of the Government. The agreement concluded in the end of 1602 between the Government and the Earl of Tyrone, as the head of the Ulster chiefs, may or may not have been made in good faith. It was one which could not, in the nature of things, last, for the rights which the chiefs claimed, and the system which their rule represented, were directly opposed to the authority of any civilised government, and rendered such government impossible. James had done good service to the cause of civilisation in Scotland when he broke the power of the Scottish nobles, put a stop to clan feuds, and instituted regular circuits for the administration of justice all over the country. It was his endeavour to carry out a similar policy in Ireland, which was, in some part at least, the reason for the discontent of the Ulster chiefs.[1] Which side

[1] Calendar of State Papers, Carew, p. xviii.

first was false to the peace, it is impossible now to say. One party declares that the chiefs began to conspire against the Government; the other, that the Government drove the chiefs to conspire in self-defence. This only is plain—that the Government was Protestant, the Ulster Irish, Catholic; that the two parties hated each other intensely; and that during these very years, all over Western Europe—in Holland, in France, and in Germany—Catholic was fighting against Protestant, or keeping truce only soon to be broken. Wherever the two religions came into contact, there was war. The Ulster chiefs began to correspond with Spain once more, as if in preparation for a new outbreak; the Government intercepted the letters, and O'Neill, Earl of Tyrone, and Macdonnell, Earl of Tyrconnel, confessed, if not guilt, at least fear of punishment, by leaving their country, and sailing from Lough Swilly, along with a number of adherents, on the 3d September 1607. The Government at once took advantage of the opportunity. It had long been the dream of the English Government to make a great "settlement" in Ulster; the whole of the governing class in England and Ireland warmly advocated the idea, because they scented plunder; and King James possessed in Sir Arthur Chichester, the Lord-Deputy, a man with vigour, ability, and determination sufficient for the task. The plan of the Plantation in Ulster bears evident marks of being the conception in its main outline and in its details of able men.

The lawyers of Elizabeth's reign had for years been labouring in order to vest in the chiefs, as personal holdings, the lands which they had formerly held—at least nominally—for the benefit of the tribes; and even those Ulster chiefs who were most opposed to English rule had taken out royal grants for their lands, though they declined to acknowledge English authority in other ways.[1] They had now rebelled against the King and been proclaimed traitors, and their lands were therefore " escheated " to the Crown. Estates were constantly changing hands in this way in Scotland during the sixteenth century. The more important of the chiefs had gone into voluntary exile with Tyrone; against the rest it was not difficult for the Crown lawyers to find sufficient proof of treason.[2] Thus all Northern Ireland—Londonderry, Donegal, Tyrone, Cavan, Armagh, and Fermanagh—passed at one fell swoop into the hands of the Crown; while, as we have seen, Down and Antrim had been already, to a great extent, taken possession of and colonised by English and Lowland Scotch. The plan adopted by King James for the colonisation of the six " escheated " counties was to take possession of the finest portions of this great tract of country, amounting in all to nearly four millions of acres; to divide it into small estates, none larger than two thousand acres; and to grant these to men of known wealth and substance. Those who accepted grants were bound to live on

[1] Calendar of State Papers, Carew, p. xix.
[2] The Plantation in Ulster, by Rev. Geo. Hill, chap. ii.

their lands themselves, to bring with them English and Scottish settlers, and to build for themselves and for their tenants fortified places for defence, houses to live in, and churches in which to worship.[1] The native Irish were assigned to the poorer lands and less accessible districts; while the allotments to the English and Scots were kept together, so that they might form communities and not mix or intermarry with the Irish. The errors of former Irish "plantations" were to be avoided—the mistake of placing too much land in one hand, and of allowing non-resident proprietors. The purpose was not only to transfer the ownership of the land from Celt to Saxon, but to introduce a Saxon population in place of a Celtic; to bring about in Ulster exactly what has happened without design during the last half-century in New Zealand, the introduction of an English-speaking race, the natives being expected to disappear, as have perished the Maori.

In 1608, a Commission, consisting of the Lord-Deputy and other well-known civilians, made a survey of the counties to be "planted," and drew up a report regarding them, which they sent over to the English Council,[2] who then proceeded to ask for offerers for the land. The description given by the Privy Council of the fertility of Ulster is preserved.[3] It paints in tempting colours the great natural capabilities of the country. It is stated that the soil is

---

[1] Calendar of State Papers, Carew, p. 154.   [2] Ibid., p. 13.
[3] Ibid., Ireland, 1608-10, p. 208.

suitable for the growth of all kinds of corn, of hops
and madder; that it is well watered and well wooded,
and its forests are accessible by water; that parts are
very suitable for the breeding of horses, and for the
feeding of sheep and cattle; and that it contains
everything needed for shipbuilding save tar.   Nor
are the sporting propensities of Englishmen forgotten,
for districts are pointed out which afford cover for
red-deer, foxes, martens, squirrels, &c.   The English Council requested the Scottish Privy Council to
draw up a list of Scotsmen willing to settle in Ulster;
and a proclamation, dated "Edinburgh, 28th March
1609,"[1] is preserved, as well as the list of the Scotsmen who had responded, each man stating the
amount of land he is prepared to take up, and giving
the name of a "cautioner," who becomes security
for the "undertaker" fulfilling the conditions of
settlement.[2]   The list is a long one, and some of the
entries amusing—Edinburgh burgesses, for instance,
having a decided "hankering" after Irish estates.
The names obtained by both English and Scottish
Councils were held over, and inquiry made regarding
the ability of the applicants to perform their contracts; eventually very few of these Scottish offerers
were accepted.   The King seems to have taken the
duty of selecting the Scottish undertakers into his
own hands, the men who got grants being of higher
social standing and wider influence than those who

[1] Register of the Privy Council of Scotland, vol. viii. p. 267.
[2] Ibid., p. lxxxviii.

first offered. A second and more careful survey having been made in 1609, the Commission proceeded,
in the summer of 1610, to divide up the land. This
second survey may have been better than the first,
but it was very inaccurate after all, as it mapped out
for division only 500,000 acres of land suitable for
"plantation," out of a total acreage of 3,800,000
contained in the six counties. What is now called
Londonderry County was reserved for the city of
London, whose different guilds undertook its colonisation. A broad tract of country was devoted to the
Church and for schools, a considerable portion for
Trinity College, and portions in each county were
laid out for the foundation of boroughs. The rest was
divided among the old proprietors, the Irish public
servants, and the English and Scottish undertakers.[1]
It is with the Scotsmen only that we are concerned.
Fifty-nine Scotsmen were chosen, and to them 81,000
acres were allotted in estates scattered over the five
counties, Londonderry, as has been said, being reserved for the city of London. A careful examina-
tion of the list of Scottish undertakers [2] enables us to
see the plan which was finally adopted for securing
proper colonists. There was, of course—as was always the case at this time—a certain number of the
hangers-on about the Court who got grants, which
they at once sold to raise money. But as a whole,
the plan of distribution was thoroughly well con-

[1] Calendar of State Papers, Ireland, 1611-14, p. 202.
[2] Hill's Plantation, chap. vii.

ceived and well carried out. It must be remembered that James I. was a clear-headed man of business when he chose to apply himself; that he was so much in earnest with regard to the settlement of Ulster, that he really did apply himself to the arrangements connected with it; and that he was well acquainted with his "ancient kingdom" of Scotland, and with its people. James seems to have seen that the parts of Scotland nearest Ireland, and which had most intercourse with it, were most likely to yield proper colonists. He resolved, therefore, to enlist the assistance of the great families of the southwest, trusting that their feudal power would enable them to bring with them bodies of colonists. Thus grants were made to the Duke of Lennox, who had great power in Dumbartonshire; to the Earl of Abercorn and his brothers, who represented the power of the Hamiltons in Renfrewshire. North Ayrshire had been already largely drawn on by Hamilton and Montgomery, but one of the sons of Lord Kilmarnock, Sir Thomas Boyd, received a grant; while from South Ayrshire came the Cunninghams and Crawfords, and Lord Ochiltree and his son; the latter were known in Galloway as well as in the county from which their title was derived. But it was on Galloway men that the greatest grants were bestowed. Almost all the great houses of the time are represented,—Sir Robert Maclellan, Laird Bomby as he is called, who afterwards became Lord Kirkcudbright, and whose great castle stands to this day; John Murray of Broughton, one of the Secretaries of State; Vans of Barnbarroch; Sir Patrick M'Kie of Laerg; Dunbar of Mochrum; one of the Stewarts of Garlies, from whom Newtown-Stewart in Tyrone takes its name. Some of these failed to implement their bargains, but the best of the undertakers proved to be men like the Earl of Abercorn and his brothers, and the Stewarts of Ochiltree and Garlies; for while their straitened means led them to seek fortune in Ireland, their social position enabled them without difficulty to draw good colonists from their own districts, and so fulfil the terms of the "plantation" contract, which bound them to "plant" their holdings with tenants. With the recipient of 2000 acres the agreement was that he was to bring "forty-eight able men of the age of eighteen or upwards, being born in England or the inward parts of Scotland."[1] He was further bound to grant farms to his tenants, the sizes of these being specified, and it being particularly required that these should be "feus," or on lease for twenty-one years or for life.[2] A stock of muskets and hand weapons to arm himself and his tenants was to be provided. The term used, "the inward parts of Scotland," refers to the old invasions of Ulster by the men of the Western Islands. No more of these Celts were wanted, there were plenty of that race already in North Antrim; it was the Lowland Scots, who were

[1] Calendar of State Papers, Carew, pp. 154, 269.
[2] Register of Scottish Privy Council, vol. ix. p. 693.

peace-loving and Protestants, whom the Government desired. The phrase, "the inward parts of Scotland," occurs again and again.

The progress of the colonies in the different counties is very accurately described in a series of reports by Government inspectors, and in the letters of Chichester himself. The Deputy believed that the "plantation" was to be the greatest blessing ever conferred on Ireland, and he did his best to make it successful. When he found that the scheme was to be thwarted in some respects, he writes very bitterly of the mistakes which the English Council was making. It had allowed far too little land to those "natives" who were willing to adopt English civilisation, and it was giving grants to men who were of no use as colonists.[1] Of the Scottish undertakers, and of the manner in which they were doing their work, there is a special report; and, on the whole, Chichester is favourably impressed with them.[2] "The Scottishmen come with greater port [show], and better accompanied and attended, but, it may be, with less money in their purses." A return is made of what work each undertaker has accomplished, and of the colonists he has brought with him. It is exceedingly interesting to note how some of the planters are proceeding vigorously to carry out the terms of their contract; others more slowly; while there are a certain number who evi-

[1] Calendar of State Papers, Ireland, 1608-10.
[2] Ibid., Carew, p. 75.

dently from the first intend to break all the conditions under which they hold their lands.   The first
class have come themselves, with their wives and
families.   They are accompanied by servants, and
by colonists to whom they have already given lands
on lease.   They have begun to build stone houses,
with fortified courts round them, called in the country
"bawns," into which cattle can be driven in cases of
alarm.   Trees have been felled, too; and, in one or
two cases, mills erected.   The tenants have not been
idle, for they have put up temporary houses, and
broken ground, and already they have taken a crop
from the ground, "and sowed oats and barley this
last year upon his land, and reaped this harvest forty
hogsheads of corn."   The stock of cattle is given
also—"70 cows brought out of Scotland, which be-
long to the tenants;" or "brought over a dozen
horses and mares for work;" or "hath 8 mares and
8 cows with their calves, and 5 oxen, with swine and
other small cattle."   The record of other planters is
not so satisfactory.   They have crossed from Scotland,
with one or two tenants, looked at the land, and
gone home again; while in one or two cases there
are entries—"has not appeared, and nothing done;"
or, "sent an agent to take possession, who set the
same to the Irish, returned into Scotland, and performed nothing."

The most interesting reports of all are those regarding undertakers who took possession in this year
(1610), made up their minds to remain and to thrive

in Ulster, and who founded families, whose names were afterwards to be well known in Ireland. In Donegal, on Lough Swilly, will be found on the map the names of two villages, Manor Cunningham and Newtown Cunningham. The men who introduced so Scottish a name into so Irish a county are thus noticed in the report of 1611 : "Sir James Cunningham, Knight, Laird Glangarnoth, 2000 acres, took possession, but returned into Scotland. Three families of British resident, preparing to build." "John Cunningham of Cranfield, 1000 acres, resident with one family of British." "Cuthbert Cunningham, 1000 acres, resident with two families of British ; built an Irish house of coples, and prepared materials to re-edify the Castle of Coole-M'Etreen ; hath a plow of garrons, and 80 head of cattle in stock." Here, too, is a delightful picture of the first settlement of one whose descendant is considered a model Irish landowner : "The Earl of Abercorne, chief undertaker in the precinct in the county of Tyrone, has taken possession, resident with lady and family, and built for the present near the town of Strabane some large timber houses, with a court 116 foot in length and 87 foot in breadth. Has built a great brewhouse without his court. His followers and tenants have since May last built 28 houses of fair coples, and before May by his tenants, who are all Scottish men, the number of 32 houses of like goodness. There are 120 cows in stock for his own use." Then here is the record of what was most probably a colony of Galloway men: " The Lo. Uchelrie [Lord Ochiltree], 3000 acres in the county of Tyrone, being stayed by contrary winds in Scotland, arrived in Ireland at the time of our being in Armagh, upon our return home, accompanied with thirty-three followers, gent. of sort, a minister, some tenants, freeholders, and artificers. Hath built for his present use three houses of oak timber—one of 50 foot long and 22 foot wide, and two of 40 foot long, within an old fort, about which he is building a bawn. There are two ploughs going upon his demesne, with some fifty cows and three score young heifers landed at Island Magy, in Clandeboy, which are coming to his proportion, and some fifteen working mares, and he intends to begin residence upon his land next spring, as he informs us."

There were many Scotsmen who were not showing the same activity as Abercorn and Ochiltree; but, in the main, they must have been the right kind of colonists; for most of them at once proceeded to build houses and provide food for themselves and their families. On the whole, the Scottish settlers seem to have done best, and the London undertakers the worst. The enthusiasm for colonisation was in exact reverse to the home comfort. The Scottish undertakers were poor men, many of them with estates deeply burdened with debt, and they belonged to a poor country. They were the men whom Scott has painted in ' The Fortunes of Nigel' They had everything to gain by going to Ulster, and so had their relatives and humbler neighbours. Besides, Ireland was only across a narrow channel, and it was a country which they could see on any clear day. If James had enlisted the men of the northwest of England to aid in the settlement of Ulster, as he did the people of the south-west of Scotland, the history of Ulster would have been materially altered. To London citizens, on the other hand, Ireland was a far-off savage country, for which they did not feel at all inclined to give up the comforts and the civilised activities of the metropolis. Thus the Londoners' colony was, for the first half-century at any rate, a failure, and the " Companies " let their lands to the " mere Irish," breaking the terms of their contract, and involving themselves in ever-recurring quarrels with the Irish authorities. One good thing the " Irish Society," which managed the London settlement, did for Ireland : it founded Londonderry and Coleraine, which in course of long years grew up to be two main bulwarks of Protestantism in Ireland.

CHAPTER IV.

THE SCOT BRINGS WITH HIM HIS SCOTTISH CHURCH.

IN this manner, during the early years of the seventeenth century — from 1606 to 1611 — there was opened up a field for emigration into which Scotsmen were to. pour during the succeeding half-century. The stream of emigrants must have varied in volume from year to year, but probably never altogether ceased; while the intercourse between the mother country and her sons in the neighbouring island was, during the whole of that period, close and intimate. Naturally, those counties which were nearest Scotland received the greatest numbers of the emigrants, until Antrim and Down contained districts as Scotch as Roxburgh or Wigtown—districts of which thirty years ago, two centuries after the emigration, a writer who knew the people well could say, these " are inhabited by a population speaking as broad Scotch as is now to be met with in the parent country, and who read and enjoy the poems of Ramsay and Burns with as much zest as

their brethren of the West of Scotland."[1]   But,
although Down and Antrim received the greatest
number of settlers, the Scots also spread into every
part of Ulster in which there was good land to be
had; or they took up their abode in the towns which
slowly began to rise round the new castle of Belfast;
at Londonderry and Coleraine, in the Londoners'
territory; and at Donaghadee, and Newtown, and
Bangor, and Lisburn, in the Scottish and English
settlements of Down and Antrim.   Probably none
of the colonies which Scotland has sent out more
deserves the support and encouragement of the
mother country than does this colony in Ulster,
for in none have the colonists had to struggle
against greater odds.   For more than a century
the Scots of Ulster were oppressed by laws which
deprived them of their civil and religious rights
and crippled their trade ; while all through the centuries they have been crushed, as they still are,
by the presence of an inferior race, whose lower
civilisation makes all their ideas of comfort lower,
and causes them to multiply with a rapidity which
ever presses on the means of subsistence.   Thus
always facing up to the savage realities of life, these
Scots of Ulster are in character more akin to our
common forefathers of the seventeenth century, retaining more of their stern Calvinism than the Scots
of this generation in the mother country.   The
establishment and growth of this Calvinistic Church

in Ireland is a remarkable chapter in the history of the Scots.

For two or three years after the "great settlement of 1610," the colony went on increasing; and then its progress was checked by rumours of a great plot among the natives to sweep away the foreign settlers. Such a conspiracy did actually exist, and was certainly a thing which might be expected; but it was dis-covered and suppressed in 1615, before it came to a head.[1]   This danger past, the settlement again made progress, the Government putting pressure on the undertakers to compel them to fulfil the conditions of their contracts, and fully plant their lands with "British" tenants.   In 1618 the Irish Government instructed Captain Pynnar to inspect every allotment in the six "escheated" counties, and to report on each one, whether held by "natives" or "foreign planters"   The report presents a very exact picture of what had been done by the settlers in the counties inspected—Londonderry, Donegal, Tyrone, Armagh, Cavan, and Fermanagh.   Pynnar points out that many of the undertakers had altogether failed to implement the terms of their agreements.   On the other hand, he reports the number of castles, "bawns," and "dwelling-houses of stone and timber built after the English fashion," and mentions the number of tenants, and the size and conditions of their holdings.   He states that "there are upon occasion 8000 men of British birth and descent

[1] Calendar of State Papers, Ireland, 1615-25, p. viii.

D

for defence, though a fourth part of the lands is not fully inhabited."[1]   Of these, fully a half must have been Scots; and if there be added the great colonies in Down and Antrim, there must have been an immigration from Scotland of between 30,000 and 40,000 in these ten years. Pynnar regrets that " many English do not yet plough nor use husbandry, being fearful to stock themselves with cattle or servants for those labours ; " and states, that " were it not for the Scottish, who plough in many places, the rest of the country might starve."[2]   When we come to the detailed report of each holding, it is easy to understand why the Scots were doing the work of colonists so well—they were led by men of energy, who were devoting their lives to the task.   Pynnar's report also enables us to understand the new framework of society which it was intended to build up in Ulster.   James and his advisers quite understood that to give a feeling of security to the new colony, it was necessary to have fortified houses all over the country, with a certain number of walled towns which should contain garrisons.   Every undertaker was therefore bound to raise a " castle of stone," which would certainly vary much in size and strength, but which was at least to give to the small settlements as much protection as did the " little towers and peels, such as are common in our Borders."[3]

[1] Calendar of State Papers, Carew, p. 422.   [2] Ibid., p. 423.
[3] Letter from Alexander Hay, Scottish Secretary of State—Privy Council Record, vol. viii. p. 793.

We have accounts of many of these castles, and of the colony which was gathering around them.

This, for instance, is a description of the settlement made in East Donegal by one of the most energetic of the Wigtownshire undertakers : " Sir W. Stewart, 1000 acres, called Rumaltho. A large and strong court 80 feet square and 14 high, four flankers, fair strong castle of same materials three and a half stories high. A large town of forty-five houses, and fifty-seven families, all British, some having estates for years. A church begun of lime and stone, built to setting on of roof. A water-mill for corn. This is a market town, and stands well for the good of the country and the King's service."[1] In County Armagh here is another very Scottish name · " Arch. Acheson, 2000 acres. A castle begun 80 feet long, 22 wide, now two stories high. Planted with British ; *in toto*, 29 tenants, with under-tenants, making 144 men with arms. Has also built a town called Clancurry, wherein dwell 29 British tenants, each having a small parcel of land—in the whole making 173 men armed."[2] The Achesons— there were two brothers among the " planters "—were from the neighbourhood of Edinburgh. Archibald was afterwards raised to the Peerage, and took his title from his property of Gosford, in East Lothian. His descendants are still Earls of Gosford. The brothers of that Sir James Hamilton who had "planted" in Down along with Sir Hugh Mont-

[1] Calendar of State Papers, Carew, p. 408.   [2] Ibid., p. 417.

gomery, also turned out most enterprising colonists. One of them, John, settled in Armagh beside the Achesons, and along with them founded "the flourishing colonies of Markethill, Hamilton's Bawn, and Mullabrack."[1] They assisted, too, in the settlement of County Cavan; Sir James "had built a very large strong castle of lyme and stone, called Castle Aubignee, with the King's arms in freestone over the gate. This castle is five stories high, with four round towers for flankers. "It stands upon a meeting of five beaten ways which keep all that part of the country." He had "settled" "forty-one families, which do consist of eighty men-at-arms."[2] Of the fortified towns, the "Londoners" were bound to erect two—Londonderry and Coleraine; and grants were given to undertakers to build forts on selected sites, round which it was intended to raise towns, like that which Lord Chichester was building round the Fort of Dungannon.[3]

The only county in which the Scottish settlers failed to take firm root was Fermanagh, for there, by 1618, when Pynnar reported, a large number of the Scottish proportions had been sold, and were held by Englishmen. The result is seen in the small number of Presbyterians in comparison to Episcopalians to be found at the present day in County Fermanagh.

It is strange to turn from these records, nearly

[1] Hill's Plantation, p. 568 note.
[2] Calendar of State Papers, Carew, p. 392.   [3] Ibid., p. 414.

three centuries old, to the political map of to-day, and compare the one with the other. It makes the reader feel how brief a period three centuries are in the history of races, and how little races change in the course of centuries. For the North of Ireland is now very much what the first half of the seventeenth century made it. North Down and Antrim, with the great town of Belfast, are English and Scottish now as they then became, and desire to remain united with the countries from whom their people spring. South Down, on the other hand, was not "planted,"[1] and it is Roman Catholic and Nationalist. London-derry County too is loyalist, for emigrants poured into it through Coleraine and Londonderry city. Northern Armagh was peopled with English and Scottish emigrants, who crowded into it from An-trim and Down, and it desires union with the other island. Tyrone County is all strongly Unionist, but it is the country round Strabane, which the Hamil-tons of Abercorn and the Stewarts of Garlies so thoroughly colonised, and the eastern portion, on the borders of Lough Neagh, round the colonies founded by Lord Ochiltree, that give to the Unionists a majority; while in Eastern Donegal, which the Cunninghams and the Stewarts "settled" from Ayrshire and Galloway, and in Fermanagh, where dwell the descendants of the Englishmen who fought so nobly in 1689, there is a great minority which struggles against separation from

[1] Knox's History of County Down, p. 17.

England. Over the rest, even of Ulster, the desire for a separate kingdom of Ireland is the dream of the people still, as it was three centuries ago. In many parts of Ireland, which were at one time and another colonised with English, the colonists became absorbed in the native population; but in Ulster, where the Scottish blood is strong, this union has not taken place, and the result is the race difference which is so apparent in the electoral statistics of the present day. It is perhaps the stern Calvinism of these Scots, which still survives, that has prevented the colony from mixing with the surrounding people, and being absorbed by them as the Jews of the northern kingdom became merged in the surrounding "heathen." The history of the Presbyterian Church is therefore an important part of the story of the Scot in Ulster; in fact, for many years the history of Ulster, as far as it has a separate history, is chiefly ecclesiastical. It must be so; for this is a story of Scotsmen and of the first half of the seventeenth century, and at that time the history of Scotland is the history of the Scottish Church. Church polity, Church observance, Church discipline, fill all the chronicles, and must have formed the public life of the people. We moderns may be extremely surprised and very much bored by the heavy polemics of these old annals; but our wonder does not alter facts, nor our disdain in all probability affect the souls of our pious ancestors.

Before glancing at the building up of the Presbyterian Church of Ireland, it is necessary to note two acts of legislation which much aided the consolidation of the Scottish colony. In 1613, after an interval of twenty-seven years, a Parliament met at Dublin, to which were summoned members from many northern towns, such as Dungannon and Coleraine, which were certainly then boroughs rather in embryo than in reality [1] This Parliament repealed a law of Queen Mary, which was intended to prevent the Scots from settling in Ireland; the Scots thus aimed at being the Western Islesmen, who infested and plundered Northern Ulster.[2] Two years later there met a convocation of clergy, which proceeded to draw up a Confession of Faith for the Episcopal Church of Ireland, as an establishment separate from that of England. The Irish clergy were at this time strongly tinged with Puritanism, and the result was that a Confession was adopted much more Calvinistic, and therefore nearer that of the Scottish Church than was the Thirty-nine Articles. The formation and growth of the Presbyterian Church was also much aided by Archbishop Ussher, the Primate of Ireland. Ussher is remembered as the most learned Englishman of a learned age; but better worth recording even than his learning is his broad-minded toleration. Unlike his contemporary, Archbishop Laud, he was incapable of rage against men who differed with him about mere forms, and ever ready to recognise the great realities in which they agreed.

[1] Calendar of State Papers, Carew, p. 170.   [2] Ibid., p. 159.

He steadily prevented all persecution of Presbyterians by Episcopal bishops, and treated the Scottish preachers as friends and fellow-Christians.[1]

There is in the Manuscript Room of the Advocates' Library in Edinburgh a quaint narrative of the history of the early days of the Presbyterian Church in Ireland, which tells how a revival of religion spread through the Scots of Ulster. Its description of the first settlers is not flattering. "In few years there flocked such a multitude of people from Scotland that these northern counties of Down, Antrim, Londonderry, &c., were in good measure planted, which had been waste before; yet most of the people, as I said before, made up a body—and it's strange, of different names, nations, dialects, tempers, breeding, and, in a word, all void of godliness, who seemed rather to flee from God in this enterprise than to follow their own mercy."[2] Probably the narrator blackened the characters of these first settlers for the purpose of heightening the effect of the mighty change which came over them. In several cases the "plantationers" came accompanied by clergymen. Both Hamilton and Montgomery looked after the spiritual wants of the emigrants in County Down, and a "minister" is stated to have accompanied Lord Ochiltree who had hereditary connections with the Presbyterian Church, his aunt

[1] History of the Presbyterian Church in Ireland, by James Reid, D.D., vol. i. p. 137.
[2] Stewart's Narrative, p. 313.

having been John Knox's second wife. There is, too, a curious record of the Bishop of Raphoe's importation of clergy from Scotland. This northern see, now styled Derry and Raphoe, was in the early years of the settlement filled by George Montgomery, a brother of Sir Hugh, the great " planter " in County Down. Bishop Montgomery held the lands assigned to his see; and we are told that he made " proclamation in the Scottish ports from Glasgow south to Larggs," " at how easy rents he would set his Church lands, which drew hither many families." [1] The colony he formed must have been considerable; for we find in 1612 that his successor, Bishop Knox, who was living on Lough Swilly, at some distance from any English garrison, obtains protection for himself and for " seven ministers that he brought out of Scotland, who are hated by the Irish." [2] The real founders of the Presbyterian Church of Ireland, however, were clergymen who took refuge in Ulster, driven from Scotland and England by the persecuting spirit then abroad against the Puritans. These men were, therefore, of necessity strong Calvinists. It must be borne in mind that the south-west of Scotland, from which the Ulster Scots largely came, was during this whole period intensely Presbyterian; it was the district from which in the succeeding generation came the " Westlan' Whigs " who fought at Bothwell Brig, and which produced the martyrs whose graves are still

[1] Montgomery MSS., p. 99.
[2] Calendar of State Papers, Ireland, 1610-15, p. 315.

visited at Wigtown, and in the quiet upland kirk-
yards of New Galloway and the "clachan" of
Dalry. The first minister to come seems to have
been Edward Brice, an Edinburgh graduate, who
settled at Broad Island in Antrim, in 1613. He
had been minister of Drymen in Stirlingshire, but
was driven from his charge by Archbishop Spottiswoode. Echlin, Bishop of Down, following the example of the Primate, made no difficulty about
recognising Brice.[1] Others, both Scottish Presbyterians and English Nonconformists, followed—
among whom one of the best known was Robert
Blair. He had been a professor in Glasgow, but
disapproving of the prelatic changes going on in
that University, he accepted the invitation of Hamilton, Lord Clannaboye, and settled at Bangor in
Down, in 1623. The story of his ordination by
Bishop Echlin shows how the spirit of Ussher was
reflected in the other bishops. Blair objected to the
" sole ordination " of the bishop, whereupon Echlin
rejoined, " Will you not receive ordination from Mr
Cunningham and the adjacent brethren, and let me
come in among them in no other relation than a
Presbyter?"[2] In this way Blair's scruples were re-
spected, and the law which imposed ordination by
the bishop of the diocese satisfied. When divines
of opposing Churches could thus agree, verily the old
chronicler was right in declaring that the " golden
peaceable age " had returned.

[1] Reid, vol. i. p. 98.   [2] Ibid., p. 103.

The Presbyterian Church rapidly strengthened, and became powerful; and the more the bishops pushed things to extremes in Scotland, the more were able men driven to take refuge in Ulster. In 1626, a son of John Welsh of Ayr, and grandson to John Knox, threw up the Chair of Humanity in Glasgow, and settled at Templepatrick in Antrim, being ordained by his kinsman Knox, who had succeeded Montgomery as Bishop of Raphoe.[1] In 1630, he was followed across by John Livingston, who was long a power in the North of Ireland. Livingston's story was similar to that of the others. He had been minister of Torphichen, and was "silenced" in 1627 by Archbishop Spottiswoode; being in Irvine during his wanderings, he was induced to go over to Ireland, where Bishop Knox acted like the Bishop of Down, and became a "Presbyter" for the nonce at his ordination.[2] In this way the Presbyterian Church of Ireland was founded by the very stoutest of Calvinists.

Meanwhile the tide of colonists flowed on. Of course there are no accurate statistics of the annual immigration, but all the records of the time speak of the West of Scotland and the North of Ireland as being united closely by daily intercourse. For instance, in 1616 there is a return among the State Papers "showing what impost was paid for wines brought into Ireland in Scottish bottoms for the year ending March 1616, more than is paid for the like

[1] Reid, vol. i. p. 112.   [2] Ibid., p. 116.

quantity imported in English and Irish bottoms."[1]
Another proof is found in the fact that the country
people were in the habit of crossing from Stranraer
to Donaghadee, attending Newtown market, selling
their wares, and crossing to Scotland again the same
night.[2]   Some years afterwards, too, when Strafford's
tyranny had driven many favourite ministers out of
Ulster, the northern Presbyterians were accustomed
to cross over to the Ayrshire and Galloway churches.
"On one occasion, five hundred persons, principally
from the county of Down, visited Stranraer to receive
the Communion from the hands of Mr Livingston."[3]

The most exact account of the emigration is contained in a very curious book of travels in Scotland
and Ireland, by Sir William Brereton, a Cheshire
man, well known afterwards in the Civil War.   He
states that he came to Irvine, in Ayrshire, on the 1st
July 1635, and was hospitably entertained by Mr
James Blair, and that his host informed him that
"above ten thousand persons have within two years
last past left this country wherein they lived, which
was betwixt Aberdine and Enuerness, and are gone
for Ireland; they have come by one hundred in
company through this town, and three hundred have
gone hence together shipped for Ireland at one tide.
None of them can give a reason why they leave the
country; only some of them who make a better use
of God's hand upon them have acknowledged to

---

[1] Calendar of State Papers, Ireland, 1615-26, p. 139.
[2] Montgomery MSS., p. 60.   [3] Reid, vol. i. p. 226.

mine host in these words, 'that it was a just judg-
ment of God to spew them out of the land for their
unthankfulness!' One of them I met withal and
discoursed with at large, who could give no good
reason, but pretended the landlords increasing their
rents; but their swarming in Ireland is so much
taken notice of and disliked, as that the Deputy has
sent out a warrant to stay the landing of any of these
Scotch that come without a certification."[1]

Thus was Ulster filled with Scotsmen, and the
simple forms of the Scottish Church established in
the North of Ireland. But the "golden peaceable
age" of Archbishop Ussher could not last long. In
1633, Thomas Wentworth, afterwards Earl of Strafford, began his celebrated term of office as Lord-
Deputy of Ireland, and with him came Laud's polity
in matters ecclesiastic. The Calvinistic Confession
of Faith was altered; the bishops tinged with Puritanism were deposed, and High Churchmen placed
in their stead; a High Commission Court was established in Dublin; and conformity to the Established
Church was enforced by pains and penalties. Then
Wentworth's hand fell heavily on the Presbyterians,
laity and clergy. Many of the latter had to flee and
take refuge in Scotland, where they again found
churches, after that country revolted against Episcopacy in 1637. Many of the laity, too, returned to
the West of Scotland, helping in this way to bind the
two countries together—Irvine, in Ayrshire, becom-

[1] Travels by Sir William Brereton (Chetham Society), p. 119.

ing a regular place of rendezvous for the Ulstermen, both lay and clerical.[1] Wentworth viewed this intimacy with a jealous eye, especially after Scotland had risen against Charles and placed an army in the field. Then the Deputy's hand fell yet heavier on the Scots of Ulster. He imposed on every Presbyterian an oath of passive obedience, long remembered as the Black Oath; he disarmed the Ulster Scots as far as he could, and raised an army of 9000 men, largely Roman Catholics, to overawe Ulster. Wentworth seems to have feared a rising of the Scots; for in a letter to Coke, the English Secretary of State, he states that there are 13,092 British men between sixteen and sixty in Ulster, but congratulates himself on the fact that they are badly armed.[2]

[1] Reid, vol. i. p. 217.
[2] Strafford's Letters, vol. i. p. 199.

CHAPTER V.

THE SCOTS AND THE IRISH REBELLION OF 1641.

THERE is mingled pain and pleasure in reading the history of the Great Rebellion, as it affected first Scotland, and then England. There is no feeling but pain and weariness for him who is so unfortunate as to be compelled to toil through the sad story of the long-drawn-out struggle, which for ten years desolated Ireland, and which needed Cromwell's iron hand and iron will to bring to an end, so that the weary wretched land might have rest. Much misery, much bloodshed the great Civil War caused in England: but it has left a glorious legacy in the memory of Cromwell's strong manhood; of Milton's noble purity of purpose and search after an ideal in politics; of the manly simplicity of many brave men who fought and died on either side — Pym, and Hampden, and Falkland; while we Scots are proud to record the intellectual greatness and moral worth of Henderson and of Rutherford, and never tire to sing the praises of that dashing cavalier, " Bonnie

Dundee." There is no silver lining to the black cloud which forms Irish history at this time; there is no name among the English and Scots who fought in Ireland which should be rescued from kindly oblivion; while the one man of pure life and principle whom the Irish put forward—Owen Roe O'Neill—lacked that strength and moral force which made men like George Washington the founders of great nations.

It is fortunately not necessary here to recount at length the horrors which characterised the revolt of the Irish in 1641, or to relate the confused story of the prolonged civil war which followed, and desolated the land. For nearly two centuries a strife of tongues has raged regarding the character of the revolt, and apologists have been found who have denied the atrocities committed on the settlers, and done their best to wipe out the bloody stain which rests on the character of the Irish people. The difficulty of arriving at the truth regarding this sad portion of Irish history is very great; for not only are the facts covered over thick with the fabrications of succeeding generations of controversialists, but even the original documents of the period are not to be trusted, many of them being framed for the purposes of deceit. Recent research has, however, proved, that while the accounts of the horrors of the revolt have been greatly exaggerated, the cruelties practised were only too horrible. This must have been so; for it is to be remembered that in Ireland it was the rising of race against race, and that the race which rose in rebellion was the lower in civilisation, and considered that it was suffering under grievous wrongs at the hands of the Government of their conquerors. Probably no fairer or more weighty account of the Rebellion of 1641 has been written than that of Mr Lecky, who says—" No impartial writer will deny that the rebellion in Ulster was extremely savage and bloody, though it is certainly not true that its barbarities were either unparalleled or unprovoked. They were, for the most part, the unpremeditated acts of a half-savage populace." [1]

Wentworth's government bore hardly on the Ulster Scots, and there are traces in his letters that he had in view a plan even more thoroughgoing than dragooning and religious persecution. He certainly did not like these Irish Presbyterians, and feared their sternness. There seems to have floated in his mind some half-formed plan of getting quit of their troubling for ever by driving them out of Ulster in a body. [2] It was not fated, however, that Wentworth was to carry out his plan; the Scots were to remain, and their stern determination to have their own way was destined to trouble the Irish dictator of the nineteenth as it had done his prototype of the seventeenth century. Wentworth was by far the ablest,

[1] History of England in the Eighteenth Century, by W. E. H. Lecky, vol. ii. p. 143. Compare also Gardiner's Fall of the Monarchy of Charles I., chaps. xv. and xvi.
[2] Reid, vol. i. p. 273.

and therefore the most dangerous, of all Charles I.'s lieutenants, and when the Long Parliament began its sittings in 1640, he was its first victim. He was impeached and executed, his death leaving Ireland really without government; for he had permitted no one near him who was capable of grasping the reins when they fell from his hands. Wentworth's rule had been hard on all—on the Roman Catholics, whether Irish or Norman-Irish, as well as on the Presbyterians, and he had given fresh sharpness and poignancy to the remembrance of the many wrongs under which they suffered. To men smarting under great grievances, the time appeared well suited for a blow for freedom. The Scottish people had just accomplished a successful rebellion, and had compelled the English king virtually to agree to all that it demanded; while England itself was evidently rapidly drifting into civil war. Ireland, moreover, was almost devoid of troops, for the army which Wentworth had raised was disbanded early in 1641; while the Government at Dublin was in the hands of two Lord Justices, lacking both character and ability. The northern settlers, besides, were without cohesion, and badly armed. The leaders of the Irish determined on a great struggle for independence. The rising was arranged with great ability, the plan being consummated largely by the aid of Roman Catholic friars, who passed from district to district unnoticed. Warning of impending danger was sent from England to the Lord Justices, but they remained unmoved;

and Dublin Castle itself would have been secured by the rebels if one of the party intrusted with its surprisal had not turned traitor on the evening before the outbreak.

It was in Ulster that the greatest fury of the rising was felt, for it was in the northern province that the land had been to the fullest extent taken from the original proprietors; religion, patriotism, and interest therefore alike called on the native population to attempt to recover supremacy. On the night of the 22d October 1641, all over Ulster, as if with one accord, the Irish rose on the English settlers, who lived in most cases in isolated farmhouses in the midst of an Irish population; while armed bodies, led by the chiefs of the Irish septs, easily surprised most of the forts, which were feebly held by small English garrisons. The plan of the original settlement had been broken through by Wentworth, when he, out of jealousy of the Presbyterians, disarmed the country, and so destroyed that system of defence which James I. had wisely judged necessary for the protection of the settlement. Before the morning broke all Ulster was ablaze with burning villages and farmhouses. There followed what must take place in every agrarian revolt—murder and outrage, even though it may have been true that "the main and strong view of the common Irish was plunder,"[1] and that the leaders, with some exceptions, deprecated murder, and desired only the expulsion of the English.

[1] Carte's History of Ormond, p. 175.

The settlers were driven out of their homes unarmed and defenceless, many of them stripped of clothing, in a singularly inclement season, with no place of refuge near at hand to which they could retreat; while around them flocked, like birds of prey, all the blackguardism of an unsettled country. It is not necessary nor desirable to describe the horrors which accompanied the flight of this miserable crowd—men, women, and children, the aged, scarce able to walk, the babe at the breast—toward the cities of refuge on the coast. None dared give them shelter or succour their distress. Many perished of cold and hunger, many were barbarously outraged and murdered; while famine and fever carried off in Dublin and Londonderry and Coleraine not a few of those who had escaped the perils of the way. One curious point it is very difficult to determine—how far the Scottish settlers suffered along with the English. It appears that the leaders of the revolt desired to distinguish between the two nationalities, probably rather to cause diversity of interest than because the Irish had reason to love Scottish more than English settlers, or because Presbyterians were more tolerant of Roman Catholics than Episco-palians.[1] It is stated by one of the bravest of the Englishmen engaged in the defence of the colony in Fermanagh, that "in the infancy of the rebellion the rebels made open proclamations upon pain of death that no Scotchman should be stirred in body, goods,

[1] Lecky's History, vol. ii. p. 130.

or lands, and that they should to this purpose write over the lyntels of their doors that they were Scotchmen, and so destruction might pass over their families."[1] This may have been the intention of the Irish leaders, but no such plan could possibly have been carried out after their followers had tasted blood, and we know for certain that many Scottish settlers perished in the uprising, while, of course, very many fell in the long civil war which followed. The Scottish settlements, as far as they escaped destruction, seem to have owed their safety to the thoroughness with which the plantation had been carried out. Thus the original Scottish colony in North Down did not suffer severely; while the settlement, by this time probably more Scottish than English, in South Antrim, and the plantation along the Foyle in Donegal and Londonderry, escaped with little injury, because in all these districts the foreign population was stronger than the native, and because the planters soon took arms in defence of their hearths and homes.

When the rebellion broke out, Charles I. was in Edinburgh, endeavouring to make terms with the Scottish Parliament, in order to separate the interests of the Covenanters from the English Puritan party. The news of the outbreak was sent to the King by Sir Arthur Chichester, Governor of Carrickfergus, and Charles read the letter to the Scottish Parlia-

---

[1] Lecky's History, vol. ii. p. 130, note.

ment on the 28th October 1641.[1] Chichester's letter, dated two days after the outbreak, announced that "certain septs of the Irish" had risen in force, and that "great fires" could be seen from Carrickfergus. The House at once appointed a committee to consider the matter, and instructed it while it awaited fuller news from Ireland to meet, that afternoon, with Lord Eglinton, and inquire "what shipping the western coast of Scotland can afford." The inquiry drew out the answer that shipping for four to five thousand men could be found from Glasgow to Ayr.[2] By 1st November the King was able to give Parliament more exact information, which he communicated in person. He read a despatch from the Lords Justices, informing him that all the north of Ireland was in rebellion; and asked the assistance of the Scottish Parliament, desiring especially their help in saving Carrickfergus and Londonderry. "The President answered, these two places did indeed very much concern the Scots, that were most numerous in the north parts of that kingdom. His Majesty replied, if he had not been a Scotsman himself, he had not spoken that."[3] The King knew that he appealed to Scotsmen as such, and that in a matter so important as the safety of their Ulster kinsmen, they would rise superior to the intense party hate which then divided Covenanters from Cavaliers.

---

[1] Balfour's Annales of Scotland, vol. iii. p. 119.
[2] Thomson's Acts of Scottish Parliament.
[3] Balfour's Annales, vol. iii. p. 129.

The Scottish Parliament was not slow in responding, for on the 3d November, only ten days after the revolt broke out, it adopted the report of the committee, which recommended that if the English Parliament would accept their assistance, and were willing to pay the troops, a Scottish force of 10,000 men should be sent into Ulster; and further, "that they should supply their brethren in Ireland with arms out of the common magazine for 3000 men, two parts muskets and the third part pikes."[1] The practical difficulty was that Ireland was a dependency of England, and that therefore the Scottish Parliament had no right to send troops without the consent of England. The force was promptly offered, but not so promptly accepted by the English Parliament, which was at this time entering on its long struggle over the Great Remonstrance.   Ireland was therefore on this occasion, as it has been so often since, sacrificed to the contention of English parties; for the English Cavaliers objected to the employment of an army of Covenanters, fearing what it might do in case of success in Ireland; while the Roundheads as strongly protested against the King being allowed to raise any other force to be sent to Ireland, in case it might be afterwards used against the liberties of his English subjects.

Meanwhile the news of the rebellion, and the reports of the atrocities attendant on it, had sent a shudder of rage and horror through Scotland, in the

[1] Balfour's Annales, vol. iii. p. 134.

same way that the tidings of the Indian Mutiny excited this country during the autumn months of 1857. The diary of John Spalding of Aberdeen, who was a kind of seventeenth-century James Boswell, and kept jottings from day to day of what struck him, is full of the prevailing feeling. His evidence is the better proof that this sympathy was universal in Scotland, and not confined to one party, from the fact that he himself was Episcopalian in his leanings, and not therefore of the party which was supreme in Parliament. " Great cruelty in Ireland, and mekill blood spilt of the English and Scottish Puritan Protestants ; fire and sword went almost through the whole land, nor mercy to sex or kind, young or old, man, woman, or child, all put to death, and their goods spoiled." [1] Again, some months later, he writes that the Irish use " fire, sword, and all manner of cruelty against man, wife, and bairn of English, Scottish, and Irish Covenanters within their kingdom, without pity or compassion." [2] The same annalist tells that on 27th February 1642, a collection was made in every parish in the kingdom for behoof of the Ulster Scots, who were forced to flee into the west parts of Scotland. He adds that out of " this poor paroche fourscoir poundis were collected." [3] This flight of great numbers of Ulster settlers into the parts of Scotland from which

[1] Memorials of the Troubles in Scotland (Spalding Club), vol. ii. p. 99.
[2] Ibid., p. 155.　　　　　[3] Ibid., p. 107.

they had emigrated, is corroborated by the Records of the City of Glasgow.   In February 1642, the Council votes a sum from the city funds for behoof of the refugees.   This not proving sufficient, on the 5th March the Corporation " ordanis ane proclamation to be sent throw the toune to desyre all these quha will give or contribut any supplie to the distressed people that com from Ireland, that they cum upon Weddnesday next at the ringing of the bells." [1]   The great excitement caused in Scotland by the rebellion in Ulster, and the intense interest shown by the country in the fate of the settlers, prove conclusively how many in every part of the mother country were personally concerned for friends and relatives among the settlers in the North of Ireland.

When at last, in the end of January 1642, terms were arranged between the English and Scottish Parliaments,[2] the Scottish authorities had no difficulty in finding at once a portion of the troops which they wished to send to Ulster.   Scotsmen had been fighting for a generation on both sides of the great Thirty Years' War, and many of these "soldiers of fortune" had returned home when the war broke out between Scotland and King Charles in 1638.   The Scottish Estates had now three regiments which had not been disbanded after the King's surrender—two stationed near Edinburgh and one in Aberdeen, where it had

---

[1] Extracts from the Records of the Burgh of Glasgow, vol. 1630-1662.

[2] Rushworth, vol. iv. p. 501.

been sent to overawe the northern Episcopalians.[1] These regiments were at once ordered to Ireland, while after the manner of the time, certain noblemen received commissions to raise other regiments to follow. There exist two most vivid sketches of the character of these troops, who were mostly professional soldiers, trained in the wars of the Continent. In Scotland they had been led against Charles by men of genius and high enthusiasm, and had behaved well; in Ireland their leaders had no spark of genius, and discipline soon became slack. We can therefore easily understand why they accomplished but little, and were not an unmixed blessing to the northern settlers. Let one of their commanding officers, Major Turner, speak for himself: " I had swallowed without chewing, in Germanie, a very dangerous maxime, which militariemen there too much follow, which was, that so we serve our master honnestlie, it is no matter what master we serve "[2]—quite the code of morals for a soldier of fortune. Here, too, is an account of how the regiment in which Turner served, Lord Sinclair's, had behaved while posted at Aberdeen: " This regiment did no good, but maikill evil, daylie deboshing, in drinking, nicht walking, combatting, sweiring, and brocht sindrie honest women servants to great misery."[3] The Scottish army of Ulster was placed under the command of David

[1] Memoirs of his own Life and Time, by Sir James Turner, p. 17.
[2] Turner's Memoirs, p. 14.   [3] Spalding, vol. ii. p. 101.

Leslie, " newly created Earl of Leven, for his successful rebellion against the King ; " and the advanced-
guard, which crossed from the western ports to Carrickfergus on the 14th April 1642, was led by his
lieutenant, Monro, who, like Leslie, and most of the
army, officers and privates, had been trained on the
Continent in the Thirty Years' War.

But long before the Scottish forces landed at Carrickfergus, the Ulster settlers had recovered from their
first panic, and had formed themselves into regiments
for mutual defence. It is a fact, that if the Irish
leaders intended to respect the lives of the Scottish
settlers, it was the latter who formed the greater portion of this militia. From the open country of
Cavan, Armagh, Tyrone, Londonderry, and Fermanagh, the rebellion swept the English and Scottish
settlers; " for the wild Irish did not onlie massacre
all whom they could overmaster, but burnt tounes,
villages, castles, churches, and all habitable houses,
endeavouring to reduce, as far as their power could
reach, all to confused chaos."[1]   Enniskillen was
saved by the bravery of its people, who again, fifty
years later, showed the stuff of which they were made.
Londonderry and Coleraine were safe, while the south
of Antrim and north of Down, and the settlement on
the borders of Tyrone and Donegal, had been rescued
from plunder. From these districts as centres the
settlers attacked the Irish. In the east, the regiments
were commanded by Chichester and Lord Conway,

[1] Turner's Memoirs, p. 19.

and by the natural leaders of the Scots, Lord Montgomery, and Hamilton, Lord Clannaboye; in the west the settlers of West Tyrone and East Donegal rallied round two very capable Scotsmen, Sir William and Sir Robert Stewart, who proved in the war that was to follow, dashing partisan leaders.[1] To these troops arms were sent by both the English and Scottish Councils, while the settlers supplemented this supply by purchasing arms. There is a proof of this in the Register House of Edinburgh, in the shape of a quaint bond, whereby Mure of Caldwell became security that his kinsman Lord Clannaboye would pay for 400 muskets at 10 pounds Scots each, which he had purchased from the "Scottish War Office."[2]

During the winter of 1641-42, these forces more than held their own against the Irish, and after Monro's arrival in April 1642, they were able, in conjunction with him, to push southwards, and retake and garrison Newry. In the west, too, the Stewarts recovered the command of much of Tyrone and Londonderry counties, and relieved Coleraine, which had been hardly pressed. Thus the principal Scottish settlements were freed, and many who had fled to Scotland, either from Wentworth's tyranny or after the rising of October 1641, began to return to Ulster. One peculiar effect the rebellion had on the North of Ireland—it swept away the Church established by law, the bishops and most of the parish clergy-

---

[1] Reid's History, chaps. vii. and viii.
[2] Hamilton's MS., p. 46.

men having perished or fled.   In its place, the Scottish army proceeded to establish a Presbyterian
Church.   It would appear that it was the custom for
each regiment to have an ordained minister as chap-
lain, and to elect from the officers a regular kirk-
session.[1] In June 1642, the clergy and elders attached
to the Scottish regiments met as a Presbytery at Carrickfergus, and, in conjunction with a number of the
Scottish residents of Down and Antrim, petitioned
the General Assembly of the Church of Scotland,
which met at St Andrews in July, to send over a
number of ministers.   The Assembly consented, and
appointed certain members who had been settled as
ministers in Ireland before Wentworth's persecution,
to proceed on a mission to Ireland.   This mission
the Assembly repeated next year; and in 1644,
a larger deputation was sent to carry the Solemn
League and Covenant to Ireland and to present it
to the people.   The Assembly's deputation on this
occasion proceeded all through Ulster, as far south as
Sligo and Enniskillen, and both troops and settlers,
English as well as Scottish, adopted the Covenant in
great numbers.[2] It is evident that the great majority
of the settlers left in Ulster were Presbyterians; for
not only would the Scots be so almost without excep-
tion, but very many of the English who had immi-
grated since 1610, belonged to the Puritan party.

Meanwhile the operations of Monro's little army
were sadly hampered for want of supplies.   It is

[1] Reid's History, vol. i. p. 370.   [2] Ibid., chaps. ix., x.

doubtful whether his force ever reached the stipu-
lated number of 10,000, although it is certain that
4000 men joined it in the autumn of 1642. The
arrangement between the two Parliaments had been
that the English should pay the Scottish troops; but
by the autumn of 1642, England was plunged in civil
war, and the money which had been raised for the
war in Ireland was seized to carry on war against
Charles.[1] The Scottish regiments, therefore, fared
very badly, and at times seem to have been driven to
live on the country in which they were settled. The
campaign of 1643 was not a brilliant one, although
ground was recovered. The winter found the troops
very discontented;[2] they had received almost no pay
since they landed, and when news came of the proposed expedition into England in support of the
Parliament, three of the regiments were no longer
to be held back, but returned to Scotland against
orders.[3] The Ulster settlers were greatly alarmed at
the prospect of being left unprotected should the rest
of the Scottish troops also go; but fortunately a supply of money and of provisions arrived at Carrickfergus in April 1644—a portion of the food being a
free gift of 3000 bolls of meal from the shire of Ayr.
About the same time, too, the Dutch showed their
sympathy with the cause of Protestantism in Ireland
by making a collection in all the churches of Holland

---

[1] Rushworth, vol. iv. p. 775.
[2] Turner's Memoirs, p. 29.
[3] Reid's History, vol. i. p. 436.

by order of the States-General: they transmitted to Ulster four shiploads of provisions and clothing, which were distributed among both people and soldiery.[1]

Thus once more Presbyterianism was re-established in the North of Ireland, and rapidly strengthened its organisation, until, in 1647, there were thirty regular congregations in Ulster.   Meanwhile the war dragged its slow length along, devastating the country horribly, and causing terrible loss of life, with changing fortune, and ever-varying parties, until Cromwell crossed in 1650, and in one dreadful campaign crushed the opposition of Catholic and Presbyterian alike, and established the rule of the English Parliament.   At first Cromwell's Government pressed hardly on the Ulster Presbyterians, and many of the settlers were scheduled for transportation into Leinster and Munster on account of their having opposed the army of the Commonwealth.[2]   Cromwell relented, however; the orders for transportation were not carried out, although lands seem to have been found for some of the Commonwealth soldiers in the northern counties.[3] Government allowances were made to the Presbyterian clergy; and under Cromwell's strict rule the North of Ireland seems to have recovered steadily from the terrible blow of the Rebellion of October 1641.

[1] Reid's History, vol. i. p. 437.
[2] Ibid., vol. ii. pp. 187 and 552.
[3] Prendergast's Cromwellian Settlement of Ireland, p. 90.

CHAPTER VI.

ULSTER FROM THE RESTORATION TO THE UNION.

THE story of the Scots of Ulster during the century and a half which succeed the Restoration would indeed be almost too dreary for a Scotsman to tell, were it not closed by the promise of brightness and prosperity in the future. It is like a day of cruel storm and grey leaden skies, which clears at sundown, with the earnest of sunshine for the morrow. The possibility of a brighter future which the Union gave, has certainly been fulfilled in Ulster. When this chapter of their history closed, the Scots of Ulster were deeply discontented, were in great measure disloyal to the Government, and desirous of a radical change of institutions; they are now among the most loyal subjects of the British Crown. The country was wretchedly poor, with waning trade and manufactures; it is now filled with a well-to-do population, while its trade and staple manufactures show what a strong race can do, even when it works under disadvantages, if it be but blessed with good government and free laws. The material prosperity of Ulster is a thing very evident; it can be proved by statistics, or seen with the eye. It shows in the humble prosperity of the small farmers of County Down, with their carefully whitewashed cottages, and their carefully tended farms, cut up with their many hedgerows; in their balances in the bank at Belfast; their belief in the Orange Society; their deep attachment to the Presbyterian Church; their supreme ambition, like their brethren in Scotland, if it be possible, to breed a son who may "wag his pow in the pu'pit." King James was right when he insisted that the colonists should be fixed to the soil by leases for long terms of years, or for life. It shows in the well-ordered little country towns, with their broad streets, and well-built churches adorned with handsome spires; their busy weekly markets; and that surest sign of a high-class population,—their well-washed, clean-pinafored children. It shows in the perfervid energy of her greater towns, especially Belfast; in the genius which their inhabitants evince for business of all kinds; in their zeal for religion,—call it sectarianism if you will, the zeal shows at least vigour and intensity; in their desire for education, which must in course of time bring culture and refinement in its train. There may be many faults of passion and headstrong zeal in this Scottish Ulster, but there is what far more than compensates, there is the first necessity for a living organism,—abounding life.

The master-mind of Oliver Cromwell grasped the

F

position in which the three kingdoms must stand if they are to remain at peace with one another, and by the exercise of his own strong, despotic will, swept away their separate Parliaments, and made them in reality one Commonwealth. The Restoration brought back their separate Parliament to Ireland as well as to Scotland; to both they were to prove a curse instead of a blessing. Fortunately for Scotland, the early years of the eighteenth century saw its Parliament ended; the nineteenth was to be begun before Ireland was united with its greater sister kingdoms. With the Restoration ceased the intimate connection which had existed between Scotland and her colony in Ulster; they had been kept together, in very great measure, by their common religion, and now in both the Presbyterian Churches fell on evil days, and had to fight a long fight for very existence. In Ireland the Scottish Church had not to wait long before it received its *quietus*. Charles II. landed at Dover on the 25th May 1660; his restoration brought back Episcopacy as a matter of course; but if the Irish bishops had been wise men it need not have brought any persecution of the Northern Presbyterians, for it was insanity for the two parties of Protestants to quarrel in face of the enormous mass of opposing Catholics. There was no Archbishop Ussher now to restrain the bishops, so they went to work with a will; and within a year of the Restoration every Presbyterian minister, save six or seven who recanted, were driven from their churches; they were forbidden to preach, baptise, marry, or exercise any function of the ministry.   The old Scottish writer Woodrow, in his 'History of the Sufferings of the Church of Scotland,' gives a list of the ejected clergy.   The numbers show approximately how the Scottish colony had recovered from the effects of the Rebellion of 1641, and grown in strength during the nine quiet years of Cromwell's government. There were in 1660, sixty-eight Presbyterian ministers in Ireland, all save one in Ulster, and of these sixty-one left their churches, and seven conformed to the Established Church [1]   Woodrow gives his reason for quoting the list : " Because I have always found the elder Presbyterian ministers in Ireland reckoning themselves upon the same bottom with, and as it were a branch of, the Church of Scotland." [2]   The Presbyterian Church in Ireland, although it soon got back its liberty to some extent, did not entirely recover the blow of 1661, until the next century was nearly run out.   The number of Presbyterian churches in Ulster gives some indication of the population of Scottish origin, although a moiety of the Presbyterians were English.   The extent of the emigration from Scotland is, however, more exactly given by Sir William Petty in his 'Political Survey of Ireland in 1672.' [3]   He takes the total population of

[1] Reid's History, vol. ii. p. 266.

[2] Woodrow's History of the Sufferings of the Church of Scotland, vol. i. p. 155.

[3] Sir William Petty's Political Survey of Ireland (London, 1719), pp. 9, 18, 20.

the country at 1,100,000, and calculates that 800,000 were Irish, 200,000 English, and 100,000 Scots,—of course the English were scattered all over Ireland, the Scots concentrated in Ulster. Petty divides the English into " 100,000 legal Protestants or Conformists, and the rest are Presbyterians, Independents, Anabaptists, and Quakers." He states distinctly that a very large emigration had taken place from Scotland, after Cromwell settled the country in 1652. The power of the Scots must, indeed, have been so considerable and so much feared as to be greatly exaggerated, for it was asserted in Parliament in 1656, that they "are able to raise 40,000 fighting men at any time."[1]

Charles II.'s reign brought many remarkable changes, which had much effect on Ulster as well as on the rest of Ireland. It saw the beginning of the " Regium Donum," the State grant to the Presbyterians. The persecution did not continue as hotly as it was begun in 1661 ; gradually the Presbyterians recovered a portion of their freedom ; gradually their ministers returned. In 1672 the Presbyterian clergy approached the King directly. The good-natured monarch received them kindly, and granted them from the Irish revenues a sum of £1200, to be given annually towards their support. It was the beginning of the State aid to the Irish Presbyterian Church, which continued with a slight interval until put an end to by the Disestablishment Act of 1869.[2]

[1] Montgomery MSS., p. 65, note.
[2] Reid's History, vol. ii. p. 334.

The other and deeper mark made on Irish history was the beginning of that repression of Irish industries which was to come into full force in Queen Anne's time. The first blow struck was an Act which forbade the exportation of cattle from Ireland to England;[1] the second, when by the fifteenth of Charles II., Ireland, which up to this time in commercial matters had been held as part of England, was brought under the Navigation Acts, and her ships treated as if belonging to foreigners.[2]

The Revolution of 1688 was accomplished almost without bloodshed in England; in Scotland the struggle really finished at Killiecrankie; in Ireland it was long and bloody. Once more it was the old race difference—a cleavage in race made more bitter by that terrible land question, the creation of the great settlements of Elizabeth and James's time, and of the yet more violent settlement of Cromwell. The Revolution in England of necessity brought civil war to Ireland. The greater portion of Ireland remained loyal to James II.; the north at once declared for William III. The Protestants of Ulster universally took arms, but their raw militia had little chance against the army which Tyrconnel, the Lord-Deputy, had got together in support of James II.[3] Rapidly he overran Ulster, until only at two points was the cause of Protestantism and of William of Orange

[1] Leland's History of Ireland, vol. iii. p. 448.
[2] Macpherson's History of Commerce, vol. iii. p. 621.
[3] Reid's History, chap. xix.

upheld—at Enniskillen and at Londonderry. It is not possible to retell the story of the heroic defence they made, for it has been told by Macaulay in a chapter among the noblest in our historical literature, and inferior pen dare not meddle with the theme.[1] It is war on a small scale, but, like the struggle of the Greeks at Thermopylæ or at Marathon, it is a fight of heroes. Nor is it necessary to recount the war by which William III. regained Ireland in 1690, save to regret that the great Dutchman's broad-minded scheme of religious toleration was not carried out, and the disgraceful repressive measures of the next reign rendered impossible. One lasting benefit William III. conferred on Ulster; he did his best to encourage the linen manufacture, especially by inducing colonies of French Protestant refugees, driven from France by the Revocation of the Edict of Nantes, to settle in north-east Ireland, with Lisburn as their centre. These Huguenots seem to have been men of skill and enterprise, many of them of rank and education. They received inducements to settle, their churches having special privileges, even when in the next reign the most severe laws were passed against Dissent.[2]

One strange memorial of this reign we have—the list of the survivors of the brave men who defended Londonderry, and who signed an address to William and Mary on the 29th July 1689, immediately after the siege was raised. The names are so strikingly

[1] Macaulay's History of England, chap. xii.
[2] See series of articles in ' Ulster Journal of Archæology.'

familiar to a Scotsman, that the list might be taken from an Edinburgh Directory. Of course there are many good English names, like that delightful surname which Thackeray has made beloved as long as the English language lasts—Dobbin; but the Scottish surnames are very numerous. There are five Hamiltons, and three Stewarts, and three Cunninghams, and three Mansons, besides representatives of very many of our Lowland Scottish surnames. One very Scottish name, too—as if to act as a commentary on the manner in which Ulster was treated in the Separation Bill of 1886—that of Gladstone, spelled in the old Scottish way, "Ja. Gledstanes."[1]

The end of the seventeenth century probably saw the last of the emigration of Scots into Ulster; while for years that were to follow the Scots were to leave Ulster in thousands for America. "For some years after the Revolution a steady stream of Scotch Presbyterians had poured into the country, attracted by the cheapness of the farms and by the new openings for trade." "In 1715, Archbishop Synge estimated that 50,000 Scotch families had settled in Ulster since the Revolution."[2] *(1688)*

We now come to two groups of measures which were to mould the history of Ireland during the eighteenth century, and whose baneful effects are still felt in the country—the repression of her woollen manufac-

[1] Walker's True Account of the Siege of Londonderry: London, 1689.
[2] Lecky's History, vol. ii. pp. 400, 401.

tures, and the penal laws in matters of religion. The
commerce of Ireland, after two devastating civil wars,
cannot have been extensive, or of a magnitude which
ought to have excited the envy or fear of England ;
but in the end of the seventeenth century the state of
England was not a prosperous one, and her woollen
manufacturers imagined that competition from Ireland
was injuring them. The consequence was that in
1698, Parliament petitioned William III. to have
laws enacted for the protection of the English woollen
manufacture by the suppression of the Irish; and
accordingly, next year Government passed an Act
through the Irish Parliament, which was utterly sub-
servient, forbidding any exportation of Irish woollens
from the country. It was afterwards followed by
Acts forbidding the Irish to export their wool to any
country save England — the English manufacturers
desiring to get the wool of the sister kingdom at their
own price.[1]

The penal laws against Roman Catholics and
Presbyterians are the special glory of Queen Anne's
time ; hers was essentially a High Church *régime*,
and in the Irish Parliament the High Church party
ruled supreme. The Acts against Roman Catholics
denied them the exercise of their worship, and laid
the great body of the people of Ireland under pains
and penalties so cruel and degrading that the laws
could not in reality be put in force to their full extent.
Those against Presbyterians were not so severe, but

[1] Lecky's History, vol. ii. p. 210.

were sufficiently galling, and strangely unreasonable, as being applied against the very men who had been the stoutest bulwark of Protestantism not twenty years before. The blow against the Protestant Dissenters was delivered through a Test Act, which compelled all serving in any capacity under Government, all practising before the law courts, all acting in any town council, to take the Communion of the Established Church. The Act at once emptied the town councils of the Ulster towns; it deprived of their commissions many who were serving as magistrates in the counties. It drove out of the Corporation of Londonderry several of the very men who had fought through the siege of 1689.[1] A strange commentary on the Test Act was given in 1715, when Scotland was in ferment owing to the Jacobite Rebellion, and trouble was feared in Ireland. The services of the Presbyterians were accepted for the militia, and then Government passed an Act of Indemnity to free them from the penalties they had incurred by serving their country and breaking the Test Act.[2]

These two groups of repressive measures fashioned the history of Ireland during the first seventy years of the last century. The country was utterly wretched, fairly broken-hearted. Its agriculture was miserable, and chronic scarcity alternated with actual famine; it had little commerce, and no manufactures, save the slowly increasing linen manufacture of Ulster. It is hard to say whether the gloom is illumined or intensified

[1] Reid's History, vol. ii. p. 511.   [2] Ibid., vol. iii. p. 69.

during the early years of the eighteenth century by the
lurid splendour of Dean Swift. His genius grasped
the facts with regard to the material needs of Ireland ;
either his madness or his clerical profession rendered
him blind to the utter barbarity of the religious position. With regard to Ulster there are two outstanding facts in her history besides the rise of the linen
manufacture—the steady emigration, and the rise of
the Secession Church. The latter is a strong proof
of the kinship to Scotland ; the former is, perhaps,
even a stronger of the blood which was in her sons,
for they left Ulster, as their forefathers had come to
it, in search of a more kindly home across the seas.
The emigration from Ulster is one of the most striking features of Irish history, and one which had a
most marked effect on the vital force of the United
States of America, which drew some of its best blood
from the Presbyterians of the North of Ireland.
There was nothing to induce the active-minded men
of the North to remain in Ireland, and they left in
crowds, going away with wives and children, never to
return. In 1718, we have mention of "both ministers and people going off." In 1728, Archbishop
Boulter states "that above 4200 men, women, and
children have been shipped off from hence for the
West Indies within three years." He regrets, too,
that almost all were Protestants. In consequence of
the famine of 1740, it is stated that for "several years
afterwards, 12,000 emigrants annually left Ulster for
the American plantations ;" while, from 1771 to

1773, "the whole emigration from Ulster is estimated at 30,000, of whom 10,000 are weavers."[1]

The Presbyterian Church in Ireland moved in parallel lines to that of the mother country during the whole of the century. There was no training college in Ireland, and most of the licentiates for the Irish Church studied at Glasgow. Naturally they took their theology from the school in which they were trained, and as it was the age of the Moderates in Scotland, so it was the time of the Non-subscribers in Ireland. In 1708, when the vials of the wrath of the High Church party were opened on the heads of the devoted Presbyterians, there were one hundred and thirty Presbyterian congregations in Ulster;[2] but there was not much life or heart in the Church. In 1726 the Non-subscribers—that is to say, the party who refused to sign the Scottish Confession of Faith—formed a separate synod, which weakened the Church and lowered its tone. Then followed in Scotland the secession of Ralph Erskine and his brethren, and in 1747 this Secession Church planted her first congregation in Ireland; soon the Isle of Saints was blessed with both Burghers and Antiburghers. These titles are but names in Scotland now, where once they were the watchwords of bitter sectarian strife. The Secession Church in Ireland, as in the mother country, was the Church of the poor;

---

[1] Lecky's History, vol. ii. p. 260. Reid's History, chap. xxvi. Froude's English in Ireland, vol. i. p. 436.

[2] Reid's History, vol. iii. p. 2.

and in Ireland the poor were so very poor, that it
was with difficulty that ordinances were kept up.
Presbyterian dissent was, in truth, the protest from
the humble members of the body, against the non-
orthodox doctrines which the "New Light" move-
ment had introduced into the Church. This con-
stant intercommunication between the Presbyterian
Churches in Ireland and Scotland is a fact worthy
of careful attention.

Meanwhile the linen manufacture was growing in
Ulster. In William III.'s time the exports amounted to £6000 annually; in 1741 they had risen to
£480,000; in 1771, to £1,691,000.[1] Then came
a check, and they fell considerably, causing great
distress among the weaving population of Ulster.
Shortly after this last date we have a very vivid and
minute picture of Ireland given in Arthur Young's
'Tour in Ireland.'[2] He visited Ulster in the years
when the American War was beginning, in the result
of which Ulster was deeply interested, for in it many
of her sons fought bravely against England; when
Paul Jones showed the weakness of England, for he
ranged the coast, and actually took a man-of-war out
of Belfast Lough.[3] Young did not find Ulster in a
very happy condition. "The increase of the people
is very great, extravagantly so; and is felt severely

[1] Macpherson's History of Commerce, vol. iii. p. 228.
[2] A Tour in Ireland, made in the years 1776-77-78, by
Arthur Young.
[3] Benn's History of Belfast, p. 620.

by emigration being stopped at present"—stopped, America being closed on account of the war. Rents were very low, " had fallen in four years 3s. an acre, and are but just beginning to get up again." The people were very poor, living chiefly " on potatoes and milk and oat bread ;" their little farms divided and subdivided until "the portions are so small they cannot live on them." In almost every cottage, from Newry northwards to Loch Swilly, he found the weaving or spinning of flax going on. "A weaver will earn from 1s. to 1s. 4d., a farming labourer 8d."

Ulster was, indeed, poor and miserable in these years. Her staple trade had suffered one of those collapses which come occasionally to all manufactures, and the exports of linen had fallen from 25,000,000 yards in 1771, to 17,000,000 in 1774.[1] Hundreds of weavers were out of work ; and to add to the misery, there had been additions to rents made on some of the great estates, especially Lord Donegal's, and many tenants were turned from their holdings.[2] The misery was greater than they could bear, and the Protestants of the North had recourse to deeds of violence. " Armed bands of misguided individuals, calling themselves ' Hearts of Oak ' and ' Hearts of Steel,' traversed the country, administered unlawful oaths, dictated terms as to rents and tithes to the proprietors, and perpetrated many other acts

---

[1] Macpherson's History of Commerce, vol. iv. p. 60.
[2] Froude's Ireland, vol. ii. p. 130.

of insubordination and outrage." [1]   On a people so
situated, the news of the Rebellion of the American
colonies had a tremendous effect, all the greater
because so many thousands had left Ulster during
the last twenty years for the American colonies, and
because so many of the " Hearts of Steel" were among
the staunchest soldiers in the American army. [2]   The
Protestants of Ulster became strongly republican, intensely sympathetic with the revolted colonies, and
sternly set on obtaining redress of their own political
grievances.   The condition of the country pointed
to the necessity for the abolition of the restrictions
on trade ; the temper of the people demanded the
abolition of the religious disabilities.   The reforms
were obtained in a strange way.   The strain of the
war with France and America compelled the British
Government to strip Ireland of troops, so that when
rumours of a threatened invasion reached the country, she seemed as if she would be an easy prey to
a French army.   The emergency roused the spirit
of the people ; and in 1778, all over the North of
Ireland, the Protestants, high and low, began to
arm and form themselves into volunteer regiments. [3]
Meanwhile the Irish Parliament, under the influence
of that group of orators whom Grattan led, awoke
out of the sleep of a century, and, close corporation
though it was, began to move for reform.   The Vol-

---

[1] Reid's History, vol. iii. p. 338.
[2] Lecky's History, vol. iv. p. 350.
[3] Froude's Ireland, vol. ii. p. 254.   Benn's Belfast, p. 630.

unteers threw their weight into the same scale, and made themselves a serious political power by uniting into a common organisation which embraced all the corps of Ulster. The Government yielded, and by a series of Acts passed through the Westminster Parliament from 1780 to 1782, Ireland was freed from the restrictions which had destroyed her woollen trade, while her shipping was accorded the same privileges as English. At the same time the penal Acts against the Catholics were abolished, and the Presbyterians were freed from the Test Act, so that public life was re-opened to them once more. This, however, did not satisfy the Ulster men. At a great assembly of delegates from the volunteer corps, representing 25,000 men, which met in uniform in the great church of Dungannon, a series of resolutions were passed demanding the independence of the Irish Parliament.[1] This, too, the Government yielded; and in 1782 there began to sit what is usually known as Grattan's Parliament.

The Volunteers reached the height of their power and fame in the Dungannon meeting; and although they intended to keep up their organisation for the purpose of retaining political power, they gradually decayed, and passed out of sight. For the rest of the century Ulster was greatly excited by political feeling, the French Revolution fanning the flame which the revolt of the American colonies had kindled. The North became mad for fraternity,

[1] Froude's Ireland, vol. ii. p. 334.

and the Society of the "United Irishmen" was inaugurated at Belfast in 1791.[1] There was to be no more Catholic or Protestant — all were to be united in one brotherhood of equality and fraternity. The Society at first embraced all who desired reform, and many of the best of the North of Ireland Presbyterians joined it; but gradually the old cleavage between Protestant and Catholic began in its midst, and as its more violent members hurried it downwards towards open rebellion, the split became wider, and in 1795 the association of Orangemen sprang into existence. In this way, when rebellion actually broke out in 1798, the struggle was not so severe in Ulster as it would otherwise have been, although much good blood was spilt of the Presbyterians of Down and Antrim. The Rebellion of 1798 brought in its train, and as its inevitable issue, the Union, which once again united the English and Scottish settlers of Ulster under a common Government with the race from which they spring. The Union rendered possible that enormous advance in contentment and prosperity which Ulster has made during this century.

[1] Benn's Belfast, p. 643.

CHAPTER VII.

THE SCOTTISH BLOOD IN THE ULSTER MEN OF TO-DAY.

IT is difficult to bring home to men who do not know Ireland and its history, the fact that there is a deep, strongly marked difference between the Ulster men and the Irish, and that that difference is not accidental, not the divergence arising out of different surroundings, not even that springing from antagonistic religious training, but is the deeper, stronger-marked cleavage of differing race. It is as distinct as that between any two varieties of any other animal—say between mastiff and stag-hound. Of course, intermarriage gradually shades off the difference of type; but take the Scots of the Ards of Down, who have probably scarcely intermarried with the Irish during the 300 years they have been in the island, and contrast them with the inhabitants of West Donegal, who have probably scarcely mixed their blood with the English, and you see the race difference. It is strange for any man who is accustomed to walk through the southern districts of Scotland, and to meet the country people going about their daily work in their everyday clothes and everyday manner, to cross into Ireland and wander through the country roads of Down or Antrim. He is in a country which is supposed to be passionately anxious to set up a separate nationality, and yet he cannot feel as if he were away from his own kith and kin. The men who are driving the carts are like the men at home; the women at the cottage doors are in build and carriage like the mothers of our southern Highlands; the signs of the little shops in the villages bear well-known names—Paterson, perhaps, or Johnstone, or Sloan; the boy sitting on the " dyke " with nothing to do, is whistling " A man's a man for a' that." He goes into a village inn, and is served by a six-foot, loosely-hung Scottish Borderer, worthy to have served " drams " to " the Shepherd and Christopher North "; and when he leaves the little inn he sees by the sign that his host bears the name of " James Hay," and his wonder ceases. The want of strangeness in the men and women is what strikes him as so strange. Then he crosses the Bann, and gets into a different region. He leaves behind him the pleasant green hills which shut in Belfast Lough, the great sweep of rich plain which Lough Neagh may well ask to show cause why it should not be annexed to its inland sea; he gets within sight of the South Derry hills, and the actors in the scene partly change. Some are very familiar; the

smart maid at his inn is very like the housemaid at
home, and the principal grocer of the little village is
the "very image" of the elder who taught him at
the Sunday-school; but he meets a donkey-cart, and
neither the donkey nor its driver seem somehow or
other to be kin to him; and the "Father" passes
him, and looks at him as at a stranger who is visiting
his town,—then the Scotsman knows that he is out
of Scotland and into Ireland. It is not in Belfast
that he feels the likeness to home so much, for everybody is walking fast just as they are in Glasgow, so he
cannot notice them particularly, and, of course, the
"loafers" at the public-house doors, who are certainly
not moving smartly, do not count for anything in either
town; but it is in the country districts—at Newtown-
Ards, or Antrim, where life is leisurely, that he recog-
nises that he is among his own people. While it is
in a town which is in the border-land between
Scottish and Irish, say at Coleraine, on a Saturday
market-day, that he has the difference of the two
types in face and figure brought strongly before him.
Some seem foreign to him, others remind him of his
"ain countrie," and make him feel that the district he
is in, is in reality the land of the Scot. The manner
in which the two races have lived side by side for
three centuries and are yet separate still, is stated
with fine courtesy and good feeling in the account
of the parish of Dungiven in Derry, written by
the rector, for an old Statistical Account of Ireland.—The book was never completed, like so

many noble attempts in Ireland.—" The inhabitants
of the parish are divided into two races of men, as
totally distinct as if they belonged to different countries and regions.   These (in order that we may
avoid the invidious names of Protestant and Roman
Catholic, which indeed have little to say in the
matter) may be distinguished by the usual names
of Scotch and Irish ; the former including the descendants of all the Scotch and English colonists
who have emigrated hither since the time of James
I., and the latter comprehending the native and
original inhabitants of the country.   Than these, no
two classes of men can be more distinct : the Scotch
are remarkable for their comfortable houses and
appearance, regular conduct and perseverance in
business, and their being almost entirely manufacturers ; the Irish, on the other hand, are more neg-
ligent in their habitations, less regular and guarded
in their conduct, and have a total indisposition to
manufacture.   Both are industrious, but the industry
of the Scotch is steady and patient, and directed
with foresight, while that of the Irish is rash, adventurous, and variable." [1]

It is not necessary to follow the history of Ulster
during the present century, for the Union brought
back the English and Scottish settlers into full communion with the great national life which they had a
right to share, and opened up to them a part in the
great future of what we lovingly call the English

[1] Statistical Account of Ireland, Dublin, 1814, vol. ii. p. 307.

nation. The legislation of 1782 and of the following session broke the shackles which had fettered hands which Nature had fashioned to be skilful in manufactures, and took away that clog on intellectual powers which were fitted to excel in commercial pursuits ; while the Union of 1801 induced these men of the North to become in very deed citizens of the United Kingdom, instead of living, as they had been wont to do, with their hearts across the Atlantic, in company with their brethren who were serving under the shadow of the Stars and Stripes. It is profitable, however, standing as we do among the closing years of the nineteenth century, to look back on the work accomplished by our kinsmen who left Scotland in the seventeenth century, and to trace the indelible marks which they have left on the " sands of time," and on the face of Ulster. And we may safely assert that they were strong men, full of firm determination and governed by deep religious feeling, because, after three centuries, their descendants bear not a few traces of the strength of character and fire of their forefathers. The Ulster of 1888 tells, deeply written across its face, the story of the emigration which began in 1606.

It is necessary to recapitulate what this emigration amounted to, and what effect it really had on Ireland. The settlement made by Hugh Montgomery and James Hamilton, in 1606, opened up the county of Down to Scottish emigrants. They took possession of the whole of the north of the county, but they

were satisfied with the arable lands which they found
there, and did not intrude on the hill-country of the
southern baronies, which therefore remained Irish
and Roman Catholic. To the west of the county
the Scots were met by the English colony which
Chichester had founded at Belfast, and which spread
up the river Lagan, along both its banks, towards
Hillsborough, on the County Down side, and far into
County Armagh on the west. Their common Puritanism formed a bond of union between these English and Scottish colonists. It made them unite and
form into communities wherever they met, whether
on the banks of the Lagan or northward throughout
the length and breadth of County Antrim, when it
was opened up to settlers by Sir Arthur Chichester
along the shores of Belfast Lough, and by Macdonnel
northward to the Giant's Causeway. The only district of this county not thoroughly colonised were
the highlands along the north-east shore. Then
came James's great scheme of colonisation in 1610,
which threw open other six counties for English and
Scottish settlers. In some of these counties, and in
some parts of them, the settlements were successful;
in others they failed to take root. In Armagh the
British colony took firm hold, because, as soon as
the county was opened up, settlers flocked into it
across the borders from Down, and in even greater
numbers from the English colony in Antrim. On
the other hand, the " plantation " of Cavan was,
comparatively speaking, a failure. In County Tyrone

the British settlers did not invade the mountainous
country on the borders of Londonderry county, but
contented themselves with the finer lands in the
basin of the Mourne, and on the shores of Lough
Neagh, and along the streams which flow into it.
Londonderry county was, during the early years of
the Settlement, left very much to itself by the "Irish
Society of London," which kept its contract largely
in the direction of drawing its rents—an operation
which is still performed by the London Companies,
the valuation of the Londoners' property being stated
in the Government return for last year at £77,000
per annum.[1]   At the mouths of the two rivers which
drain the county, however, the London Society
founded the towns of Londonderry and Coleraine,
and these as time went on became ports by which
emigrants entered and spread all over the fertile
lands of the county.   In Donegal the British only
attempted to colonise the eastern portion; while
in Fermanagh the Scots seemed to be so little
at home that they handed over their lands to the
English, who here established a strong colony,
from which have sprung some of the best-known
names among the English in Ireland.   Into these
districts of Ulster both English and Scottish emigrants, but especially the latter, continued to stream
at intervals during the whole of the seventeenth
century.

The two counties which have been the most

[1] Thom's Irish Almanac, p. 736.

thoroughly transformed by this emigration are the two which are nearest Scotland, and were the first opened up for emigrants. These two have been completely altered in nationality and in religion. They have become British, and in the main, certainly Scottish. Perhaps no better proof can be given than the family names of the inhabitants. Some years ago, a patient local antiquary took the voters' list of County Down " of those rated above £12 for poor-rates,"[1] and analysed it carefully. There were 10,028 names on the list, and these fairly represented the whole proper names of the county. He found that the following names occurred oftenest, and arranged them in order of frequency—Smith, Martin, M'Kie, Moore, Brown, Thompson, Patterson, Johnson, Stewart, Wilson, Graham, Campbell, Robinson, Bell, Hamilton, Morrow, Gibson, Boyd, Wallace, and Magee. He dissected as carefully the voters' list for County Antrim,[2] in which there were 9538 names, and found that the following were at the top : Thompson, Wilson, Stewart, Smith, Moore, Boyd, Johnson, M'Millan, Brown, Bell, Campbell, M'Neill, Crawford, M'Alister, Hunter, Macaulay, Robinson, Wallace, Millar, Kennedy, and Hill. The list has a very Scottish flavour altogether, although it may be noted that the names that are highest on the list are those which are common to both England and Scotland ; for it may be taken for granted that the English

---

[1] Ulster Journal of Archæology, vol. vi. p. 77.
[2] Ibid., p. 323.

"Thompson" has swallowed up the Scottish "Thomson," that "Moore" includes the Ayrshire "Muir," and that the Annandale "Johnstones" have been merged by the writer in the English "Johnsons." One other point is very striking — that the great Ulster name of "O'Neill" is awanting, and also the Antrim "Macdonnel." The scrutiny was in-teresting, too, as showing that certain peculiarly English and Scottish surnames of less frequency were localised in certain parishes, and only found in these ; a colony had settled on that spot in the seventeenth century, and there their descendants remained. Taking Down and Antrim together, twenty-five surnames covered 17 per cent of the population. Another strong proof of the Scottish blood of the Ulster men may be found by taking the annual reports presented to the General Assembly of the Presbyterian Church of Ireland, held in June 1887. Here are the names of the men, lay and clerical, who sign these reports, the names being taken as they occur : J. W. Whigham, Jackson Smith, Hamilton Magee, Thomas Armstrong, William Park, J. M. Rodgers, David Wilson, George Macfarland, Thomas Lyle, W. Rogers, J. B. Wylie, W. Young, E. F. Simpson, Alex. Turnbull, John Malcolm, John H. Orr. Probably the reports of our three Scottish Churches taken together could not produce so large an average of Scottish surnames.

Perhaps the most characteristic outcome of the

Scottish colonisation of Ulster is the Presbyterian Church of Ireland. Its career since the Union has been highly honourable, and one which gives promise of good work in the future; for it has been steadily consolidating, and closing its ranks, in presence of the great masses of its opponents. In 1818, a union was brought about between the two bodies of non-conforming Presbyterians who bore the quaint Scottish titles of Burghers and Anti-burghers, and they became a "Secession Church"; in 1840, this Secession Church made up its differences with the main body of Presbyterians, and formed the Presbyterian Church of Ireland. The United Church has since gone on striking its roots deeper and deeper into Ulster society. The Disestablishment Act of 1869 put an end to the Regium Donum—the grant to the Presbyterian Church, begun by Charles I. This endowment had been given, with one slight break, every year since its institution, had been frequently increased, and in the last year it was voted, amounted to £39,000. The clergy who had received allowances from the Regium Donum were, however, entitled to allowances for life; these as a body they commuted for a slump sum, and handed over to the Church the sum of £587,735, to form a permanent endowment for the Presbyterian Church of Ireland. The interest of this sum has been supplemented by a Sustentation Fund.

The Presbyterian Church of Ireland now numbers over 550 congregations, and there are, besides, small

United Presbyterian and Reformed Presbyterian Churches.[1] The Presbyterians number over half a million—about one-tenth of the population of the country. The Episcopalian Church claims over 600,000. The Presbyterians may with safety be taken as representing with sufficient accuracy the Scots of Ulster. The manner in which the Presbyterians are distributed is itself sufficient proof of this. Ulster claims fifteen-sixteenths of them, and they are found just where we know that the Scots settled. In Antrim they constitute 45 per cent of a total population of 422,000; in Down, 40 per cent of a population just under 300,000; while in Londonderry they are 33 per cent; in Tyrone, 19; and in Armagh, 16 per cent of the population. But it is when we come to examine the details of the census of 1881 that the clearest traces of the Scottish emigration are to be found. Down has only 40 per cent of Presbyterians, but that is because the south of the county was never colonised, and is still Roman Catholic. The old Scottish colony in Upper Clannaboye and the Great Ards is still nearly as Presbyterian as in 1630. It has already been recorded how James Hamilton, immediately after settling in 1606, raised churches and placed "learned and pious ministers from Scotland" in the six parishes of his estate—Bangor, Killinchy, Holywood, Ballyhalbert, Dundonald, and Killyleagh. These parishes have gone on flourishing, so that when

[1] Report of the Presbyterian Church of Ireland, 1887.

the census collector did his rounds through Hamilton's old estate in 1881,[1] he found that it contained 29,678 inhabitants; and that although it was situated in what has been called the most Catholic country in Europe, only 3444 Roman Catholics were there to be found, as against 17,205 Presbyterians. For two centuries and a half these "Westlan' Whigs" have stood true to their Scottish Church. The record of Hugh Montgomery's settlement is quite as curious. His old headquarters, Newtown-Ards, has grown into a flourishing little manufacturing town; and Donaghadee is a big village well known as a ferry for Scotland. Still they remain "true blue" Presbyterian. Montgomery's estate is pretty well covered by the four parishes of Newtown-Ards, Grey Abbey, Comber, and Donaghadee. These have a united population of 26,559; the Presbyterians number 16,714, and the Roman Catholics only 1370—the balance being mainly Episcopalians and Methodists. In Armagh and in Fermanagh, on the other hand, the Episcopalians are more numerous than the Presbyterians. In the former there are 32 per cent belonging to the Church of Ireland, and only 16 to the Presbyterian Church; while in the latter there are only 2 per cent of Presbyterians, as against 36 of Episcopalians. The balance of nationalities and of religions remains to all appearance what the colonisation of the seventeenth century made it, and that

[1] Detailed Census of Ireland, 1881, County Down.

notwithstanding the great emigration from Ulster
during the eighteenth century. The only strange
change is, that Belfast, which was at its foundation
an English town, should so soon have become in
the main Scottish, and should remain such unto
this day.[1]

The most outstanding feature of Irish industry is
the linen manufacture. In this the Scots have done
their full share of work, although it cannot be said
that they have any right to claim any exclusive credit
for its present importance. It is indeed altogether
the creation of the colonists, but English and French
have contributed their share as well as the Scots. It
is only right to bear testimony to the debt of gratitude
due to the Huguenot refugees, who seem to have
possessed rare mechanical genius. The descendants
of these French settlers are among the most honoured
of the Protestants of the North. The linen trade of
Ireland is now one of the important industries of the
United Kingdom ; it is almost entirely confined to
Ulster ; and a glance at the list of the members of the
" Linen Merchants' Association of Belfast " will con-
vince the most sceptical how thoroughly the captains
of the industry are English and Scotch. According
to the factory inspector's reports for 1885, 61,749
persons were employed in the flax mills and factories
in Ireland.[2] Of these the greatest number were in

---

[1] Benn's Belfast, p. 88.
[2] Twentieth Annual Report of the Flax Supply Association,
Belfast, 1888.

County Antrim—the great town of Belfast bringing up the total; Armagh comes second; Down third, with Londonderry and Tyrone far behind; and the other counties of Ulster represented to a very small extent. The supremacy of Ulster in the linen manufacture is shown in a very striking way by taking the statistics for 1885 for the United Kingdom. Of the total of 1,155,217 spindles used in the spinning of linen in the United Kingdom, 817,014 were in Ireland, as against 220,644 in Scotland and 117,559 in England; while of 47,641 power-looms employed in the trade of the United Kingdom, 21,954 are in Irish mills. The application of steam-power to the weaving of linen may be said to be the work of this generation of Ulster men, as in 1850 there were only 58 power-looms in Ireland, although steam-power had been already extensively introduced into Scotland and England. It is pleasant to know that Ulster retains her supremacy for the quality of her linens, as well as for the quantity produced.

But the linen manufacture is also a blessing to the North of Ireland from the stimulus it gives to her agriculture, by encouraging her farmers to grow the flax which the factories spin and weave into linen. The acreage under flax has varied much from year to year; in 1887 it stood at 130,202, almost entirely in Ulster, and the value of the flax produced was nearly one million sterling. As four times this quantity is consumed in the United Kingdom, a wide margin for profitable increase is still left to the agriculturists of

Ulster. Of the Irish counties, Down heads the list for the production of flax, with Tyrone and London-derry as second and third. It is a crop which scourges the ground, and requires good farming, but in successful years it is exceedingly profitable.

In other commercial pursuits besides the linen trade, the descendants of the Scottish settlers have shown themselves worthy of the stock from which they spring, and have made Ulster a striking con-trast from its wealth and prosperity to the other provinces of Ireland. The great town of Belfast is a most remarkable example of what energy and ability can do. A century ago, it was a small town of 12,000 inhabitants; it is now a handsome, thriving city of near 300,000. Besides its great linen trade, it is one of the most frequented ports in the United Kingdom. " Its custom dues are larger than either Glasgow or Hull, being surpassed only by London and Liverpool in the United Kingdom."[1] Its repu-tation for shipbuilding is rapidly extending, and at the present time there are in course of construction on the banks of the Lagan, what promise to be two of the greatest and swiftest ships of our mercan-tile marine. Into other branches of industry these Scots of the North of Ireland are throwing them-selves with perfervid energy and wonderful success. Meanwhile the city is extending its arms down both sides of Belfast Lough ; it has cut new streets through

[1] Article on "Situation in Ireland," 'Scotsman,' 16th Jan-uary 1888.

old quarters, built handsome public buildings, inaugurated new drainage works, and is at the present
time forming a new sea-channel three or four miles
long through the shallows of the Lough.   The success of Belfast is not due to the salubrity of its
climate, to the richness of the soil, or to its natural
position, certainly not to the small stream which
forms its harbour.   There are many towns more
advantageously situated in Ireland.   The increasing
prosperity is the well-merited reward of the work of
her sons, and her condition is widely different from
that of the other great towns of Ireland, because her
inhabitants differ in race from theirs.

It is, indeed, in the practical work of the world
that those men of Ulster excel at home and abroad.
They have made but little mark in art or literature;
but in commerce and manufactures and science, in
war and diplomacy, they have done their own share
of hard and successful labour.   Americans have ever
been willing to bear testimony to the part which
Ulster men took in building up the fabric of the
United States.   The Presbyterian emigrants were
among the stoutest soldiers who fought in the War
of Independence; and many of the best citizens
of the United States spring from the same stock.
Descendants of Ulster men have filled the President's
Chair in the persons of James Monroe, James Knox
Polk, John C. Calhoun, and James Buchanan; Stone-
wall Jackson came of the same blood; and A. T.

Stewart, who founded in New York the greatest business in the world, was from County Down. Ulster has produced three men who have in a notable way translated science into practice: Fulton, one of the inventors of steam navigation; Morse, whose name is linked with telegraphy; and M'Cormick, the inventor of the reaping-machine. To the service of this country she has given many who have upheld the honour of England as soldiers and administrators. Ulster can boast of the names of some of the best of the captains who served under Wellington; and she gave to India two men who helped materially to save her for England during the great Mutiny— Henry and John Lawrence. Of the blood of the settlers also sprang Lord Castlereagh and George Canning, Sir Henry Pottinger and Lord Cairns; and also one of the most brilliant and successful of living administrators, Lord Dufferin, who is the inheritor of the title of one of the first of the Scottish settlers, James Hamilton, Lord Clannaboye, and is the possessor of part of the old Scottish settlement on the south shore of Belfast Lough.

In literature and art these Scots of the North of Ireland cannot rival their brethren of the old land. Perhaps their history during the century and a half which succeeded the Restoration sufficiently accounts for their want of the power of expression in prose or verse, in sculpture or in painting; for during that period the North of Ireland was wretchedly

H

poor, and its Presbyterian inhabitants were by the Test Act cut off from the higher culture of the universities. Certainly the names which Ulster has produced in literature and art cannot rival the great men which she has brought forth for the active pursuits of life :—

> "He came from the North, and his words were few;
> But his voice was kind and his heart was true."

But though these men of Ulster are not much given to the arts of poetry or oratory, still they are a strong practical race, full of energy, courage, and perseverance, who, if allowed fair-play, will leave the world a little better than they found it. They have had a hard fight for existence during the centuries they have been in Ireland; and now when they have begun to enjoy the full fruits of the Union of 1801, we need not wonder if they protest, not loudly but deeply, against any attempts to impair the arrangement which has brought to them good government and prosperity. Time will, we trust, help to bridge over that deep chasm which separates the Scot and the Irish in Ireland; but the cleavage is more likely to be closed if they both continue to live in the full communion of that great empire in which both may well glory. Certainly it seems little short of madness in any statesman to attempt to force a race so "dour" and determined as are these Ulster men— descended as they are from blood as "dour" as any which the world has known, the English and Scottish Covenanters who fought together at Marston Moor —to attempt to compel men of such a stock to submit to a form of government against which they protest, and which they dislike and distrust with all the force of their nature.

THE END.

PRINTED BY WILLIAM BLACKWOOD AND SONS.

OURE TOUNIS COLLEDGE.

SKETCHES OF THE HISTORY OF THE OLD COLLEGE OF EDINBURGH.

WITH AN APPENDIX OF HISTORICAL DOCUMENTS.

Crown 8vo, 5s.

SOME OPINIONS OF THE PRESS.

Spectator.

" Mr Harrison has not only searched to much purpose the old Scotc burgh records and other sources of information for the history of th foundation of the University, but has given a very careful account o its history to the days of Principal Robertson, accompanied by pic tures of Edinburgh society about the close of the eighteenth century His narrative is clear, flowing, and commendably succint."

Literary World.

"With a love-inspired patience and diligence he has sought out anc studied historical documents, exploring all manner of out-of-the-wa stores of information, and skilfully weaving all his discoveries into most attractive and readable book."

Bibliographer.

"Mr Harrison tells the history of the College well, and leads u along from the day of small things to the distinguished success of later date with a tale of unflagging interest."

Scotsman.

"It contains a series of pictures of episodes in the past life o Edinburgh, painted by one who is thoroughly familiar with his sub ject, and whose sympathy with it is as sincere as his knowledge is exhaustive."

Midland Counties Herald.

"Mr Harrison, who was evidently in love with, and possessed competent knowledge of his subject, has related the history of th College with a crispness and vivacity of style which are calculate not only to commend it to Scotchmen, but to secure for it the atten tion of a wide circle of readers."

WILLIAM BLACKWOOD & SONS EDINBURGH AND LONDON.

LATELY PUBLISHED.

ON SOME OF SHAKESPEARE'S FEMALE CHARAC
TERS. By HELENA FAUCIT, LADY MARTIN. Third and
Cheaper Edition. With Portrait. 8vo, 7s. 6d.

"This is one of the books we dare hardly criticise.......We have seldor
met with a book which has given us more refined enjoyment as we read, an
more original matter for meditation afterwards."—*Times.*

THE LAND BEYOND THE FOREST. FACTS, FIGURES
AND FANCIES FROM TRANSYLVANIA. By E. GERARD, Autho
of 'Reata,' 'Beggar my Neighbour,' &c. In Two Volumes, wit
Map and Illustrations. 25s.

"She has given a delightfully varied and interesting, and, for general infoi
mation, sufficiently complete account of the 'Land beyond the Forest.' Th
book is more readable than most fiction."—*Scotsman.*

TIMAR'S TWO WORLDS. By MAURUS JOKAI. Author
ised Translation by MRS HEGAN KENNARD. Crown 8vo.

"It is long since we met with a story so vigorous—so full of human syn
pathy, of strength and pathos.......We regretfully close this delightful book.
—*Saturday Review.*
"Not only as its author's masterpiece, but as a masterpiece of Europea
literature, pervaded by a primeval freshness of style that should titillate th
palate of the most jaded novel-reader."—*Athenæum.*

FRAGMENTS FROM MANY TABLES. BEING TH
RECOLLECTIONS OF SOME WISE AND WITTY MEN AND WOME
By GEORGE RUSSELL. Crown 8vo, 4s. 6d.

NEW AND CHEAPER EDITION.
WANDERINGS IN CHINA. By C. F. GORDON CUMMIN
Author of 'At Home in Fiji,' 'A Lady's Cruise in a French Mar
of-War,' 'Fire Fountains,' &c., &c. With Portrait of the Autho
and numerous Illustrations. Complete in One Volume, 8vo. 10

INSULINDE. EXPERIENCES OF A NATURALIST'S WIFE I
THE EASTERN ARCHIPELAGO. By MRS H. O. FORBES. Pos
8vo, with a Map, 8s. 6d.

"A sober, gracefully written narrative."—*Westminster Review.*
"An unpretending but pleasantly written description of everyday life in th
Eastern Archipelago. The volume might very well serve as a guide-boo
for those whose vocation may take them into those yet little-known spot
of the earth's surface."—*Vanity Fair.*

A NEW AND CHEAPER EDITION OF
POOR NELLIE. By the Author of 'My Trivial Life an
Misfortune.' New Edition. Crown 8vo, 6s.

"It is a very powerful and remarkable book."—*Spectator.*
"A work of great ability and of absorbing interest."—*St James's Gazette.*

THE BLACKSMITH OF VOE. A Novel. By Paul
CUSHING, Author of 'Misogyny and the Maiden,' 'A Woman with a Secret,' &c. 3 vols. crown 8vo, 25s. 6d.

"Full of clever drawing, and rich in striking incident."—*Daily Telegraph*.
"It is a powerful and interesting novel, which should increase the reputation of its talented author."—*Scotsman*.

EPISODES IN A LIFE OF ADVENTURE ; or, Moss
from a Rolling Stone. By LAURENCE OLIPHANT, Author of 'Piccadilly,' 'Altiora Peto,' 'Haifa,' &c. New Edition. Post 8vo, 6s.

"The book is written in a most pleasing style, and is fresh and vigorous throughout."—*Spectator*.
"The book bristles with adventures in every page. Among these his sporting reminiscences will be found the most absorbingly exciting. We wish we could transcribe some of them."—*Saturday Review*.

LAYS OF THE SCOTTISH CAVALIERS, and Other
Poems. By Professor AYTOUN. Printed from a New Type, and tastefully bound in cloth, fcap. 8vo, 3s. 6d. Cheap Edition, in paper cover, 1s.

"A delightful edition of the beautiful ballads of Professor Aytoun.......
Many will delight in obtaining in so handy and portable a form the romantic and stirring poems which have helped to make the name of Professor Aytoun a household word with us."—*Morning Advertiser*.
"Finer ballads than these, we are bold to say, are not to be found in the language."—*Times*.

SARACINESCA. By F. Marion Crawford, Author of
'Mr Isaacs,' 'Dr Claudius,' 'Zoroaster,' &c. Third Edition. Crown 8vo, 6s.

"'Saracinesca' is a very remarkable book, and a great advance upon any of the author's previous works."—*Academy*.
"It is a book of which even the greatest masters of fiction might with reason have been proud."—*Pictorial World*.
"No better picture has been drawn of Roman society than the one contained in Mr Crawford's new novel 'Saracinesca.'"—*Morning Post*.

A New and Cheaper Edition. Complete in One Volume.

GEORGE ELIOT'S LIFE. As related in her Letters
and Journals. Arranged and Edited by her Husband, J. W. CROSS. New Edition, Illustrated, with Portrait and Wood Engravings. Crown 8vo, 7s. 6d.

NOVELS BY GEORGE ELIOT. Cheaper Editions.
Crown 8vo, with Illustrations. Viz. :

Adam Bede, 3s. 6d.—The Mill on the Floss, 3s. 6d.—Felix Holt, the Radical, 3s. 6d.—Scenes of Clerical Life, 3s.—Silas Marner, 2s. 6d.—Romola, with Vignette, 3s. 6d.—Daniel Deronda, with Vignette, 7s. 6d.—Middlemarch, with Vignette, 7s. 6d.

DATE DUE

UNIVERSITY PRODUCTS, INC. #859-5503

BOSTON COLLEGE LIBRARY
UNIVERSITY HEIGHTS
CHESTNUT HILL, MASS.

Books may be kept for two weeks unless otherwise specified by the Librarian.

Two cents a day is charged for each book kept overtime.

If you cannot find what you want, ask the Librarian who will be glad to help you.

The borrower is responsible for books drawn in his name and for all accruing fines.